Human Rights and Literature

Pramod K. Nayar

Human Rights and Literature

Writing Rights

palgrave
macmillan

Pramod K. Nayar
University of Hyderabad
Hyderabad, India

ISBN 978-1-137-50431-9 ISBN 978-1-137-50432-6 (eBook)
DOI 10.1057/978-1-137-50432-6

Library of Congress Control Number: 2016958035

Printed on acid-free paper

This Palgrave Macmillan imprint is published by Springer Nature
The registered company is Nature America Inc.
The registered company address is: 1 New York Plaza, New York, NY 10004, U.S.A.

Preface

The turn to literary texts and discourses in this book is one that has been, in some sense, in the offing for some years now, with concerns over the aesthetic, narrative and representational strategies appropriate to the task of documenting Human Rights violations occupying centre stage in numerous essays and my earlier book, *Writing Wrongs: The Cultural Construction of Human Rights in India* (2012).

Political commentaries and legal discourses do not provide, in my view, the adequately robust scaffolding to construct the subject, the person, of human rights. Literature which, as Geoffrey Harpham reminded us years ago, has always been concerned with the Other, offers a key route into the very idea of the human and insights into those excluded from this idea. It is this view of the literary that produced *Human Rights and Literature Writing Rights.*

Hyderabad, India Pramod K. Nayar

Acknowledgments

This book, which took me into literary texts remarkable for their representations of human courage and human brutality and of suffering and silences, would not have been possible but for the support system I inhabit. The 'thank yous' expressed here are woefully minimal for what the members of this system do.

Rachel Krause of Palgrave Macmillan tracked me down and invited me to submit a proposal—which was the motivation for actually cobbling together the preliminary plans for this book. To Rachel, the driving engine of *this* construction, I am very grateful.

My parents and parents-in-law, Nandini and Pranav, provide the immediate setting in which I work—their support remains as reliable as ever. Pranav's comment, 'Oh, you are again reading novels about torture and genocide?—what horrible reading!' deserves special mention here.

Friends who provide online entertainment and enquire about work and health deserve huge thanks: Josy Joseph, V. Premlata, Ibrahim Ali, Walter Perera, Ajeet Dumpala, Soma Ghosh, Achamma Tarun ('Chechu'), Rebecca Tarun ('Ron') and Vaishali Diwakar. To Neelu who ensures that subjects far from human rights and torture *do* exist in my life with her endless supply of jokes: thank you very much for the necessary distraction.

To K. Narayana Chandran for his phenomenal insights into critical theory and literature, his scholarship, evident even in routine conversations, that enables me to make connections between texts and themes, and above all for his indulgent support at the workplace, I owe more than I can state in a few words here.

Nandana Dutta who has been, in her own words, struggling to keep up with all that I write, was passionately enthusiastic about this book from its very inception. She has helped me with critical texts, offered suggestions and insightful comments on those parts of the work I sent her. Thank you, Nandana.

Parts of this book, especially the sections on witnessing in fictional representations were delivered in the form of a valedictory address, 'Differentiated Similitude, The Continuum of Suffering and the Transnational Literature of Human Rights', at the International Conference on 'Transnational Approaches in Literary Studies', Department of English, Anna Adarsh College, Chennai, on January 28, 2016. I thank Archana Sardana of the English Department for the invitation to speak. Sections of the book will also appear in the essay 'The Human Rights Torture Novel: Unmade Subjects, Unmaking Worlds', in *Orbis Litterarum* in 2016–2017. I am grateful to the referees of this essay for helping me improve it considerably and, indirectly, this book itself.

I should, at the risk appearing self-promotional, record that this book has benefited from journal reviewers who have sharpened my essays in the field over the last few years. I thank in particular the editors and reviewers of *Ariel*, *South Asian Review*, *Rupkatha*, *South Asian Film and Media*, *Postcolonial Text*, *Journal of Postcolonial Writing*, *Indian Journal of Gender Studies* and *Journal of Commonwealth Literature*. To Om Dwivedi and Julie Rajan for inviting me to contribute to *Human Rights in Postcolonial India* (2016)—thank you.

To Sara Crowley Vigneau, Connie Li, Bradley Showalter at Palgrave Macmillan for their work on this book, many thanks.

Anna Kurian, First Reader, was thrilled at the very idea of this book and completely pleased when she read the full manuscript. How many of the ideas do you think, Anna, came out of our discussions over the years? For her companionship, her loyal affections and critical eye that demands—and crafts—better writing from me—inexpressible, unquantifiable gratitude. As for the query from some students as to whether she does inscribe 'ouch' in the margins of my manuscripts at places of bad writing: yes, she does!

Elizabeth Goldberg, whose work over the years has enabled me to find my way through the thicket of the field 'Human Rights and Literary Studies', cheerfully agreed to write the endorsement. For her commitment, her writing and her encouragement, her gifts of books, I owe a great deal.

Contents

Introduction: The Literature of Human Rights

Beliefs and aspirations about what the human *means*, *ought to* mean and *deserves*, acquire currency through cultural texts wherein models of the human, the abhuman and the subhuman are drawn. Cultural texts construct a social imaginary—the set of beliefs, ideologies and aspirations—of the human, and by extension, of Human Rights. Sophie McClennen and Joseph Slaughter put it forcefully: 'legal scholars and practitioners would do well to recognize that human rights are a cultural discourse as much as they are a set of legal standards' (2009: 6). Cultural discourses and their texts, in many media forms and genres, tell stories of what it means to be human or to be denied humanity, and of these storytelling forms, Literature is by far the most pervasive.

Literature rationalizes in and through its wide variety of narratives what it means to be human. Such a *narrative* tradition is crucial, for, as Human Rights scholar Anthony Langlois sees it, 'human rights ... are rights, generated by narratively rationalized metaphysical beliefs, beliefs, which inform us as to what the metaphysical category "human person" means' (2005: 383). In the social and political realms, Human Rights campaigns also require that stories—especially of Rights being denied—be told: 'human rights work is, at its heart, a matter of storytelling' (Dawes 2009: 394). Scholars foregrounding the centrality of *stories*—both telling and listening—to the work of Human Rights pay particular attention to fiction in which idea(l)s of the human subject are debated (Slaughter 2007; Dawes 2007; Anker 2012). Others believe that *listening* to such stories is essential for Human Rights. Literature, specifically fiction, Amnesty International declares, has a key role in developing empathy: 'Reading fiction develops our empathy and social understanding. Empathy helps us stand up to prejudice and discrimination' (http://www.amnesty.org.uk/literature-and-human-rights#.VkLiiL8wCzQ. 11 Nov. 2015). 'All stories', write Kay Schaffer and Sidonie Smith, 'invite an ethical response from listeners and readers' (2004: 4). Such stories have 'strong affective dimensions … affects that can be channelled in negative and positive ways, through personal, political, legal, and aesthetic circuits that assist, but can also impede, the advance of human rights' (4–5). Nationally organized political projects such as the Truth and Reconciliation Commissions in South Africa, Guatemala, Chile, Argentina and Rwanda are exemplars of particular forms of storytelling (Payne 2008). Such projects also have fiction set around them (Graham 2003; Gready 2009; Bartley 2009) and are a part of this apparatus of the Human Rights campaign.

For their role in Human Rights campaigns, more and more literary (and cultural) texts have been brought into the study of representations and discourses of rights, of which more recently we can think of, besides the ones listed above, Elizabeth Swanson Goldberg (*Beyond Terror* 2007) and anthologies such as *Theoretical Perspectives on Human Rights and Literature* (2012), *Teaching Human Rights in Literary and Cultural Studies* (2015) and *The Routledge Companion to Literature and Human Rights* (2016). Energizing Human Rights through literary readings and using Human Rights norms to read literary texts, argue Elizabeth Swanson Goldberg and Alexandra Schultheis Moore, not only shape new directions in 'the republic of letters' but also 'bring the interpretative methodologies of literary criticism to bear on human rights to uncover the stories that normative rights discourses implicitly include and exclude' (2012: 3).

Literature constitutes a dominant cultural discourse and a set of texts within which particular beliefs about what it means to be human may be found. This discourse might take one of two critical routes into examining and defining normative ideas of the Human.

The first route consists of a narrative tradition where the Human's growth and development is documented. Lynn Hunt's work on the sentimental novel and Joseph Slaughter's on the *bildungsroman* demonstrate how specific literary forms generate and resonate with ideas of the Human in cultural, economic and political discourses. Slaughter proposes that *bildungsroman* and HR 'both articulate a larger discourse of development that is imagined to be governed by natural laws and that is historically bound to the modern institutions and technics of state legitimacy' (2007: 93). The emphasis here, clearly, is on genres in which the Human *emerges*. To imagine the human is to imagine Human Rights.

The second route establishes a narrative tradition where, in sharp contrast to the first, a broken, deprived, dehumanized subject might be found. It concerns itself with those expelled from the very category of the Human. 'Literature as a genre seems especially committed to an exploration of outsiderhood,' wrote Geoffrey Galt Harpham, well before the arrival of an 'interdiscipline' called Human Rights and Literature (1999). Since 'conceits of human dignity and bodily integrity simultaneously require for their legibility the threat of bodies being violated, broken, and defiled,' often, HR discourses rely upon such bodies to underscore the conditions under which some bodies are rendered outside the pale. Thus, the idea of human dignity may only be highlighted implicitly, by pointing to 'inverse images of corporeal unmaking and abuse' (Anker 3–4). In a later essay, speaking of Jamaica Kincaid's protagonist, Xuela, Anker asks: 'how should we understand the formative role of loss and brutality in her account of herself?' (2016: 38). This second tradition is concerned with contexts and environments inimical to the making and survival of subjects and is as crucial to the understanding of Human Rights as the first.

This book extends the work on Literature and Human Rights from Joseph Slaughter, James Dawes, Lynn Hunt (2007) and others, but in a direction suggested by Harpham's and Anker's proposition. It examines texts that are 'strong, emotive stories often chronicling degradation, brutalization, exploitation, and physical violence; stories that testify to the denial of subjectivity and the loss of group identity' (Schaffer and Smith 2004: 4). It deals with literary texts where the human subject's social ontology is eroded and which therefore implicitly demonstrate how the subject can only develop and grow in *conditions* that *sustain* life—and in many parts of the world such conditions are rare. Unlike the *bildungsroman* the torture novel and the genocide novel focus on precarity, and conditions in which individuals and communities are excluded from the very category of 'human'. Legal subjectivity itself, Wendy Hesford reminds us, is 'predicated on the hierarchy of vulnerability and victimization' (2016: 73).

Torture, extended periods of deprivation and genocide are also ways of thinking about the human. The 'persuasiveness of torture as a rhetorical device', writes Jennifer Ballengee, 'plays upon specific notions of human mortality and related notions of the *human*' (4, emphasis in original). The torture novel shows the demolition of the possibility of the human subject by showing the destruction of human corporeal integrity. The sentimental terror novel, such as Yasmina Khadra's, examines the dehumanization of humans as terrorists (McManus 2013). Other cultural texts, closely aligned with the torture *novel*, document similar dehumanizations, albeit in disturbingly graphic detail. Stephen Eisenman has this to say about cultural texts of torture:

> The torture photographs from Abu Ghraib precisely enshrine objectification and heteronomous thought: the idea that certain people by virtue of race, religion, nationality, gender or sexual preference may be denied rights to basic freedoms of action, association and thought (or even to life itself), and that the greatest ethical imperative is to follow orders. The Abu Ghraib pictures represent a moral universe in which people are used as mere (disposable) means to ends. (14)

The argument applies to the torture or genocide novel just as well, if we consider Alan Cumyn's *Man of Bone*, Edwidge Danticat's *The Farming of Bones* or Michael Ondaatje's *Anil's Ghost*: all novels that speak of the impossible objectification and dehumanization of humans. Such texts demonstrate how the demolition of the human is made possible through specific social, economic and political discourses that circulate anterior to the events and justify the events afterwards. The contemporary 'torture turn' in the 'war on terror', for instance, had a discursive prologue, tracked painstakingly through a mountain of documentation by Karen Greenberg et al. in *The Torture Papers*. When the USA declared some Arabs/Afghanis/Iraqis 'enemy combatants', it was *representational* manoeuvring that enabled it to deny 'prisoner-of-war' rights mandated by the Geneva Conventions to the prisoners at Abu Ghraib and Gitmo. The categorizing and labelling of specific communities such as Jews, Africans or specific castes in India as subhuman, in *cultural texts*—of which Literature is one kind—right from India's ancient and Europe's Early Modern period, enabled the making of laws, the institution of slavery and genocides. There is a representational or discursive anterior to events and actions such as genocide. Anthropologist Nancy Scheper-Hughes, examining what she calls the 'genocide continuum', writes:

> The [genocide] continuum refers to the human capacity to reduce others to nonpersons, to monsters, or to things, that give structure, meaning, and rationale to everyday practices of violence. It is essential that we recognize in our species (and in ourselves) *a genocidal capacity* and that we exercise a defensive hypervigilance, a hypersensitivity to the less dramatic, *permitted*, everyday acts of violence that make participation (under other conditions) in genocidal acts possible, perhaps more easy than we would like to know.

> I would include all expressions of social exclusion, dehumanization, depersonalization, pseudo-speciation, and reification that normalize atrocious behavior and violence toward others. (2002: 369, emphasis in original)

Expressions of exclusion and dehumanization in cultural texts—literature, film, popular cultural forms—that reflect the larger genocide continuum 'fix' humans in specific categories that then enable the violation of their subjectivity, identity and bodies. Thus 'symbolic forms, societal contexts and representational meanings are intimately tied to relations of power' and 'political representations and the politics of representation' force us to pay attention to not only the 'intersections between culture and law, but also to the ways that these discourses make and unmake meaning' (McClennen and Slaughter 7).

A discourse of exclusion and dehumanization is thus central to the genocide continuum, and a preliminary to the act of genocide. Studies of the Holocaust and other genocides have documented the discourses that preceded and accompanied acts of extreme violence on specific groups and communities. Dehumanization enabled the perpetrator to 'ignore or reject the particularity of each and every person' in favour of a conceptualization as 'the Jew' or 'the Tutsi' (Byrd 2013: 108–109. Also Savage 2013). Rowan Savage puts it thus: 'dehumanization is not an accompaniment to, but a fundamental aspect of genocide' (140), and might be defined as 'a discourse constructing the legitimate use of organized violence toward civilian groups' (140). It is 'a mechanism that imposes degrading attributes on both individuals and entire groups for purposes of massive group destruction, the defining feature of genocide' (Hagan and Rymond-Richmond 2008: 877).

Such studies underscore language and representation as integral not only to the defining of the Human but also as a key element in both discourses and practices—the genocide continuum—where such a (normative) human is violated. Underscoring the role of the *language* of Human Rights, Sophia McClennen and Joseph Slaughter write:

> Human Rights are the proper name of a particular set of promises about a future of social equality and justice, about the "advent of a world in which human beings shall enjoy freedom of speech and belief and freedom from fear and want," as the preamble to the Universal Declaration of Human Rights (UDHR) articulated in 1948. This means that there is always a gap between the imagination of human rights and the state of their practice. (4)

'Proper names' and 'promises' are articulated within the lives of characters and the plots of literary texts, in the voices of the ones whose bodies have been violated and who carry scars of loss, absence and rejection. Dehumanization is also, in the case of Dalit texts from India, the effect of structural conditions of exclusion, marginalization and oppression.[1] This thinking through of the *representational* moves leading to the 'end' of the human requires an examination of the kind of texts that form the groundwork of this book. In such texts we are called upon to imagine the Other, the one outside the pale of Human Rights.

Such an outsider or the Other to the Human might be found in literary texts from around the world. In the twentieth century, postcolonial studies have expended considerable energies on Euro-American texts that have encoded the exclusion of some collectives from the category of the Human. Critical Race Studies has demonstrated how specialized discourses and their literary expressions have consigned Jews, Africans and others to perpetual 'outsiderhood'. But texts that speak of outsiderhood are not necessarily postcolonial in origin or confined to Africa, South America or Asia, as this book shows. Atrocities and violations of the Human are similar even if they are not identical, and the denial/deprivation of HR is to be treated as equivalent if not equal. This book proposes that HR texts, rooted in contexts as disparate and discrete as Sarajevo and Rwanda, with characters as diverse as tortured Tutsi and raped Korean comfort women, might be profitably and sympathetically read within a frame of 'differentiated similitude' (Rothberg 2011: 528). It does not present a hierarchy of victims or perpetrators, and assumes that suffering *can* be compared and rights denied through various modes which can be located together on a continuum.

This book places texts from around the world on such a continuum of suffering.

***

While fiction remains the dominant genre in this work, poetry and drama also figure wherever relevant.

Chapter 1, 'Unmade Worlds', proposes that HR Literature places the HR subject within a genocidal imaginary where a process of dehumanization works to erode the subjectivity of the individual. It studies HR texts that foreground the *contexts* in which subjects lose their subjectivity. HR texts are interested in the *emplacement* of subjects in order to examine the conditions in which it is not possible to remain an autonomous, coherent and agentic subject. Texts such as Boubacar Diop's *Murambi, The Book of Bones*, Chris Bohjalian's *Sandcastle Girls*, Edwidge Danticat's *The Farming of Bones*, Dave Eggers' *What Is the What* and Ondaatje's *Anil's Ghost* focus on rumours and fugitive discourses that construct the 'outsider' who is then placed on the genocidal continuum to be exterminated. The chapter's sections, organized around fugitive discourse and the genocidal imaginary, the making of a 'moral vacuum' and a 'new social order' that then facilitates both demonization and infrahumanization, study the discursive and narrative construction of worlds within nation-states in which specific ethnic groups and sections of the citizenry are rendered disposable.

Chapter 2, 'Unmade Subjects' argues that HR Literature is more often than not expressive of an anxiety over the destruction of the subject. This destruction of the subject is mapped out in the theme of the unmaking of bodies and the worlds in which the bodies are embedded. Within HR Literature, the theme of unmade bodies, inverted selves and unliveable worlds is most forcefully articulated in the 'HR torture novel', of which the chapter analyzes Alan Cumyn's *Man of Bone*, J.M. Coetzee's *Waiting for the Barbarians*, Lawrence Thornton's *Imagining Argentina*, Gillian Slovo's *Red Dust*, Achmat Dangor's *Bitter Fruit*, Farnoosh Moshiri's *The Bathhouse*, Vyvyane Loh's *Breaking the Tongue* and Omar Rivabella's *Requiem for a Woman's Soul.* They are novels that show us violated bodies and eroded subjects, dehumanized individuals and collapsed everyday worlds. In its sections on painful bodies, debased subjectivity and proximate grief the chapter shows how tortured and debased bodies destroy the 'home' of the subject of HR. Proximate grief goes some way towards empathetic understanding and the minimal restoration of a sense of self, but this process, as several novels show, is riddled with potential risks.

In Chap. 3, the focus is on novels such as *Red Dust*, Tony Eprile's *The Persistence of Memory*, *Anil's Ghost*, *Imagining Argentina*, David Park's *The Truth Commissioner* and others that deal with witnessing. HR Literature represents certain individuals who find a means of retrieving subjectivity through a narration of their dehumanization. With sections on witnessing and generation of heteropathic empathy, knowledge production, trauma-memory citizenship and political subjectification, the chapter demonstrates how witnessing is the key process in the rebuilding of subjectivity after the confinement, torture and dehumanization of the human.

Chapter 4 addresses the collective in HR texts. With sections on 'zones of indistinction', communities built around mourning and the making of 'counterpublics', the chapter studies the genocidal continuum in numerous HR novels. Such a continuum mobilizes people to participate in the extermination campaign. The novels studied here include texts that thematize mass suffering and mourning: *The Cellist of Sarajevo*, *Sandcastle Girls*, *Imagining Argentina*, *Of Love and Shadows*, *In the Shadow of the Banyan*, *The Farming of Bones*, among others.

Bibliography

Anker, Elizabeth S. 2012. *Fictions of Dignity: Embodying Human Rights in World Literature*. Ithaca and London: Cornell University Press.

Anker, Elisabeth S. 2016. "Commonly Human": Embodied Self-Possession and Human Rights in Jamaica Kincaid's *The Autobiography of My Mother*. In *The Routledge Companion to Literature and Human Rights*, ed. Sophia McClennen, and Alexandra Schultheis Moore, 37–45. New York: Routledge.

Bartley, Aryn. 2009. The Violence of the Present: *David's Story* and the Truth and Reconciliation Commission. *Comparative Literature Studies* 46(1): 103–124.

Byrd, Dustin. 2013. Neither Man Nor Beast: Dehumanization in Direct and Systemic Violence. *memoria ethnologica* nr. 48–49. An XIII: 105–118.

Dawes, James. 2007. *That the World May Know: Bearing Witness to Atrocity*. Cambridge, MA: Harvard University Press.

Dawes, James. 2009. Human Rights in Literary Studies. *Human Rights Quarterly* 31(2): 394–409.

Graham, Lucy Valerie. 2003. Reading the Unspeakable: Rape in J.M. Coetzee's *Disgrace*. *Journal of Southern African Studies* 29: 433–444.

Gready, Paul. 2009. Novel Truths: Literature and Truth Commissions. *Comparative Literature Studies* 46(1): 156–176.

Goldberg, Elizabeth Swanson. 2007. *Beyond Terror: Gender, Narrative, Human Rights*. New Brunswick: Rutgers University Press.

Goldberg, Elizabeth Swanson, and Alexandra Schultheis Moore. 2012. Introduction: Human Rights and Literature: The Development of an Interdiscipline. In *Theoretical Perspectives on Human Rights and Literature*, eds. Elizabeth Swanson Goldberg and Alexandra Schultheis Moore, 1–16. New York: Routledge.

Hagan, John, and Wenona Rymond-Richmond. 2008. The Collective Dynamics of Racial Dehumanization and Genocidal Victimization in Darfur. *American Sociological Review* 73: 875–902.

Harpham, Geoffrey Galt. 1999. *Shadows of Ethics: Criticism and the Just Society*. Durham and London: Duke UP.

Hesford, Wendy S. 2016. Contingent Vulnerabilities: Child Soldiers as Human Rights Subjects. In *The Routledge Companion to Literature and Human Rights*, eds. Sophia McClennen and Alexandra Schultheis Moore, 69–77. New York: Routledge.

Hunt, Lynn. 2007. *Inventing Human Rights: A History*. New York: WW Norton.

Langlois, Anthony J. 2005. The Narrative Metaphysics of Human Rights. *International Journal of Human Rights* 9(3): 369–387.

McClennen, Sophia A., and Joseph Slaughter. 2009. Introducing Human Rights and Literary Forms, or, the Vehicles and Vocabularies of Human Rights. *Comparative Literary Studies* 46(1): 1–19.

McClennen, Sophia, and Alexandra Schultheis Moore. 2016. Introduction: Aporia and Affirmative Critique. In *The Routledge Companion to Literature and Human Rights*, eds. Sophia McClennen and Alexandra Schultheis Moore, 1–19. New York: Routledge.

McManus, Anne-Marie. 2013. Sentimental Terror Narratives: Gendering Violence, Dividing Sympathy. *Journal of Middle East Women's Studies* 9(2): 80–107.

Payne, Leigh A. 2008. *Unsettling Accounts: Neither Truth Nor Reconciliation in Confessions of State Violence*. Durham and London: Duke University Press.

Rothberg, Michael. 2011. From Gaza to Warsaw: Mapping Multidirectional Memory. *Criticism* 53(4): 523–548.

Savage, Rowan. 2013. Modern Genocidal Dehumanization: A New Model. *Patterns of Prejudice* 47(2): 139–161.

Schaffer, Kay, and Sidonie Smith. 2004. *Human Rights and Narrated Lives: The Ethics of Recognition*. London: Palgrave Macmillan.

Scheper-Hughes, Nancy. 2002. Coming to Our Senses: Anthropology and Genocide. In *Annihilating Difference: The Anthropology of Genocide*, ed. Alexander Hinton, 348–381. Berkeley and Los Angeles, CA: University of California Press.

Slaughter, Joseph R. 2007. *Human Rights, Inc.: The World Novel, Narrative Form and International Law*. New York: Fordham University Press.

Note

1. 'Dalit' is a term now used to describe castes and communities previously called 'untouchables' in India. In the Hindu hierarchy of castes, they occupy the lowest rungs. They practice specific forms of labour (dealing with, say, leather, which so-called upper castes will not handle), and are severely poor. With affirmative action they have begun to acquire education and move into government jobs.

CHAPTER 1

Unmade Worlds: Emplacement

In Polish poet Aleksander Wat's horrific 'Imageried'Epinal', he describes a girl who is being comforted by her father's executioner. The father's decapitated head is later 'washed', 'nicely painted' and placed on a pole. The poem concludes:

> With that pole she marched in a parade on a sunny, populous road,
> Under her school placard:
> "Happiness to all—death to enemies"
>
> (in Forché 1993: 413)

The girl is drafted, either voluntarily or involuntarily, into the propaganda in so effective a manner that she holds up her father's decapitated head as an endorsement of the state's slogan. The girl forsakes her filial connections for the state's rhetoric, abandons her mourning for sloganeering. A particularly horrific instance in literature where the subject loses her filiation but also loses her *sense of loss*, Wat's poem captures the centrality of context in Human Rights (HR) texts.

HR literary texts foreground the contexts in which subjects lose their subjectivity, the conditions that enable the taking away of their identities through the breaking of their bodies and the inflicting of loss and indignities. HR texts are interested in the *emplacement* of subjects in order to examine the conditions in which it is not possible to remain an autonomous, coherent and agentic subject. In HR literature therefore, with its interest in the subject of Human Rights and the person who might bear

P.K. Nayar, *Human Rights and Literature*,
DOI 10.1057/978-1-137-50432-6_1

the legal and moral weight of rights, there occurs considerable emphasis on the worlds inhabited by subjects.

In HR texts, the emplacement is one of crisis, of dehumanization and discrimination. Bryan Turner proposes:

> Human rights abuses disconnect and destroy the conditions that make embodiment, enselfment, and emplacement possible. They typically involve some attack on the body through torture and deprivation, an assault on the dignity of the self through psychological threat, and some disruption to place through exclusion—imprisonment, deportation, seizure of land, or exile. (27)

Subject worlds are the worlds embedding the individual, and which begin to break down resulting in the concomitant breakdown of the individual. 'Unmade worlds' in the chapter's title is intended to capture worlds that are unmade but also worlds that contribute to the unmaking of subjects.

Thus, it is not the perpetrator-victim model of HR violations that this chapter is interested in. Rather, it is the set of conditions—material, discursive, legal, social and economic—that enables the emergence of a perpetrator and of the oppressor to perform certain actions directed at destroying the subjectivity of another by capitalizing on the vulnerability of this other.

Adriana Cavarero has argued that while all of us are vulnerable as humans, only some of us are helpless, and she points to babies, the infirm and the old as instances of the latter. HR literature offers us a set of themes in which the vulnerability of the individual or group is exposed and broken wide open as a mode of inducing the destruction of the subject/s. In its focus on the emplacement of subjects, HR literature highlights conditions in which life is not liveable (Butler 2009).

Jean Améry writes that we need

> an element of trust in the world, and in our context what is solely relevant, is the certainty that by reason of written or unwritten social contracts the other person will spare me-more precisely stated, that he will respect my physical, and with it also my metaphysical, being. The boundaries of my body are also the boundaries of my self. My skin surface shields me against the external world. If I am to have trust, I must feel on it only what I *want* to feel. (28, emphasis in original)

As a result of this lack of respect, indeed violation, of the surface, or what he calls 'the border violation of my self by the other' (33), the tortured, says Améry, 'can no longer feel at home in the world' (44). Améry is proposing, I suggest, that once the first home, the bounded body, has been broken into, it becomes impossible to be at home anywhere else. Reinhold Görling argues that torture is the very negation of *sociality* because it destroys the very foundations of an individual's subjectivity: her or his openness to the world.

But exactly how does the set of conditions in which such a collapse of the foundations of subjectivity come about? How does the sociality of the human erode so that the sociality is founded on pain, suffering and loss rather than on mutually constitutive dependency? HR literature suggests that in specific contexts a genocidal imaginary emerges that then not only justifies but *demands* the erosion of social ties. The genocidal imaginary is the discursive and narrative construction of worlds within nation-states in which specific ethnic groups and sections of the citizenry are portrayed as disposable subjects, as the abject.[1]

I use 'genocidal' to indicate the *move* towards mass extermination, a tendency and imaginary that by constructing specific models of Otherness *could* lead to mass killings. It is the manufacturing of conditions in which such extermination might be legitimized and sanctioned. Studying the genocidal imaginary is an analysis of the contexts in which the destruction of human subjects, and therefore the denial of rights, exists as potential. The genocidal is the expulsion of peoples, groups and identities from the mark of the human. This expulsion might take the form of disappearances, expropriations and, in extreme cases, massacres and mass killings. Disappearances, as seen in novels set in Argentina or Chile (*Imagining Argentina*, *Naming the Spirits*, *Of Love and Shadows*) empties a city, region and society of so-called subversives. The genocidal imaginary here assigns a specific set of attributes to people and professions (journalists, for instance). Massacres and ethnicides are the most obvious manifestations of the genocidal imaginary and are examined in texts like Boubacar Diop's *Murambi, The Book of Bones*, Chris Bohjalian's *Sandcastle Girls*, Edwidge Danticat's *The Farming of Bones*, Dave Eggers' *What is the What* or Ondaatje's *Anil's Ghost*. War is the large-scale expression of the genocidal imaginary, cast as an extreme condition. Expropriations are the deprival of possessions, from body to names to identities (*ex-proprius*) that we see in numerous texts like *The Bathhouse* or *Imagining Argentina*. In other cases, such as Dalit writing from India, structural inequalities ensure that some segments of society are perpetually denied basic rights and dignity. For instance, a Dalit woman who has had her entire family wiped out by the Sasmals, upper-caste landowners, is forced into prostituting herself for the same men in Manoranjan Barman's 'Shabori'. Now Shabori's emplacement in the caste-ridden, poverty-stricken world of her village may not be akin to war, but the expropriation of all that constitutes human life and dignity is not radically different from the conditions in which the young boys of Sudan live in Eggers' novel. Not only is Shabori forced into prostitution to the very men who killed her family, she is mocked for this state of affairs by the village. Her caste ensures the extinction of her family, and her gender ensures continuing exploitation. As a man who witnesses the deal struck between Shabori and the Sasmals says: 'They [the Sasmals and Shabori] don't eat together because she is "untouchable", but sleeping together does not create any problems!' (2012: 111).

The genocidal imaginary with its effective Othering manifests in HR literature most explicitly in the theme of dehumanization. Dehumanization, scholars point out, enables individuals to perpetrate extreme violence upon helpless victims because of their (perpetrators') emotional detachment (Lang 2010). When humans are dehumanized, wrote Herbert Kelman in an early essay, 'principles of morality no longer apply to them and moral restraints against killing are more readily overcome' (1973: 48). Some have proposed that social distance determines the severity of dehumanization perpetrated by one group on another (Haagensen and Croes 2012). Dehumanization enabled the perpetrator to 'ignore or reject the particularity of each and every person' in favour of a conceptualization as 'the Jew' or 'the Tutsi' (Byrd 2013: 108–109. Also Savage 2013: 143). Narrative dehumanization, in numerous cases, is the preliminary moment to genocides. Rowan Savage puts it thus: 'dehumanization is not an accompaniment to, but a fundamental aspect of genocide' (140), and might be defined as 'a discourse constructing the legitimate use of organized violence toward civilian groups' (140). It is 'a mechanism that imposes degrading attributes on both individuals and entire groups for purposes of massive group destruction, the defining feature of genocide' (Hagan and Rymond-Richmond 2008: 877).

This chapter proposes that HR literature places the HR subject within a genocidal imaginary where a process of dehumanization works to erode the subjectivity of the individual. If, as Anthony Langlois (2005) claims, HR discourses are founded on a narrative tradition where the human is defined, genocidal discourses construct the human whose rights might be denied—an inverted subject of Human Rights, so to speak.

Dehumanization, writes Johannes Lang, 'would involve a unilateral denial of subjectivity in the other in a way that would disqualify the victim as someone who could engage with, or affect, the perpetrator's own subjectivity' (228). That is, dehumanization destroys the intersubjective foundations of sociality and thereby the social ontology of the individual. Dehumanization consists of a refusal to recognize the 'human' qualities of others, an association of the other with negativity, an essentializing of this other ('The Jew', 'The Tutsi') and the amplification of the other-as-threat. Dehumanization might also take the form of an infrahumanization, the reduction of the human to subhuman or animal states in the perpetrator's discourse. Collectively, then, dehumanization seeks to evoke feelings and responses of condemnation, disgust and hostility (Byrd). Dehumanization is a set of discourses and representations, the invocation of emotional regimes of hatred and distrust through speech and imagery that offer the perpetrators the justification for their acts. Genocide becomes a legitimate solution to a perceived problem—a problem presented through the discourses of Othering.

HR literature posits the existence of a moral vacuum in which victim and perpetrator are *emplaced*. Once such a moral vacuum is in place as a context of social relations it enables dehumanization and infrahumanization. But both the moral vacuum and the dehumanization are preceded, or on occasions accompanied, by a specific form of 'fugitive' discourse: rumours. Worlds occupied by the subjects of HR begin to be unmade first through rumours about imminent invasion, purges and assaults.

Fugitive Discourse, Rumour and the Genocidal Imaginary

In *The Farming of Bones*, Edwidge Danticat has a woman ask: 'You heard the rumors? ... They say anyone not in one of those Yanki cane mills might be sent back to Haiti.' To this the Dominican-born woman responds anxiously: 'Me, I have no paper in my palms to say where I belong. My son, this one who was born here in this land, has no papers in his palms to say where he belongs' (69).[2] Later the rumours are of a different order: 'Many had heard of groups of Haitians being killed in the night because they could manage to trill their "r" and utter a throaty "j" to ask for parsley, to say perejil. Rumors don't start for nothing, someone insisted' (114). Then the rumours about killings increase (114, 125, 126, 208). In *Murambi*,

Gasana notes how his girlfriend, Marie-Hélène, always 'alludes to the stories of rape [of Tutsis by the Hutu militia, to which Gasana belongs]'.

In both these instances, the victim and perpetrator—the Haitians and the Tutsis as victims, the state's armed forces and Hutus as perpetrators in the two novels—have their identities and character sketches fixed in unverifiable stories and rumours. Further, the social relations between Dominicans and Haitians, Hutus and Tutsis are themselves embedded in the typified identities constructed within unsubstantiated stories. Rumour, clearly, has political functions in the social order because, as we can see, it organizes the collective perceptions about races and tribes as potential *oppressors* and *victims*. There are the threats and there are the likely, or intended, victims, all constructed within the fugitive discourse of hearsay, rumours and stories.

Rumour, like gossip, is 'fugitive speech' because it reveals 'layers of lived experience and thus embedded affect that are otherwise occluded from view' (Derby 2014: 132). It is usually 'unsanctioned' (131). Rumour's 'intersubjective, communal adhesiveness' constitutes its enunciative dimension and its performative dimension lies in its ability to circulate like a 'contagion' (Bhabha 2009: 286). Rumours are characterized by a certain 'indeterminacy of meaning' (288). Their role in social relations is crucial because they

> cannot be regarded simply as a response to or a trigger of conflicts and violence; rather, they are constitutive of them, particularly in the formation of a common moral imagination and in shaping the social interactions between the conflicting parties. (Espeland 2011: 20)

These fugitive speech acts are instrumental in constructing political identities outside the traditional modes: 'Through rumors, groups perform disidentifications and reidentifications outside of the scope of authenticity and rationality under which political identities are traditionally cast' (Moulin 2010: 349). Further:

> Rumors arise from ambiguous situations. They come to life as people try to understand events, facts, or perceptions that are unclear, unsaid, uncertain in the face of weak information. For those involved, rumors become a way to fill in the gaps and to suggest particular understandings of events within a community. Therefore, rumors tell us more about social perception than about notions of truth or validity. (351)

Thus rumours construct identities, determine social relations and offer interpretive frames for events and processes by relying on an indeterminacy of meaning and the concomitant generation of effects like panic or anxiety. They draw upon mythic histories and invented pasts on occasion as a mode of defining the crisis in and of the *present*. They help define Otherness.

In HR literature rumours are discursive acts of cultural framing that construct Otherness, invoke ancestral rivalries and spread stories about killings. Rumours eddy around both victims and perpetrators and are constitutive of their identities in the context of social relations with other tribes, races and identities.

The entire machinery of the Empire in *Waiting for the Barbarians* begins to move because of stories in circulation. The Magistrate records:

> But last year stories began to reach us from the capital of unrest among the barbarians. Traders travelling safe routes had been attacked and plundered. Stock thefts had increased in scale and audacity. A party of census officials had disappeared and were found buried in shallow graves. Shots had been fired at a provincial governor during a tour of inspection. There had been clashes with border patrols. The barbarian tribes were arming, the rumour went; the Empire should take precautionary measures, for there would certainly be war. (8–9)

That the Empire's actions might be founded on absolute falsehood—not very different from events in our own times when mythical 'data' about 'Weapons of Mass Destruction' helped initiate war—is brought home to us in the very next statement made by the Magistrate:

> Of this unrest I myself saw nothing. In private I observed that once in every generation, without fail, there is an episode of hysteria about the barbarians. There is no woman living along the frontier who has not dreamed of a dark barbarian hand coming from under the bed to grip her ankle, no man who has not frightened himself with visions of the barbarians carousing in his home, breaking the plates, setting fire to the curtains, raping his daughters. These dreams are the consequence of too much ease. Show me a barbarian army and I will believe. (9)

Eventually, when the Magistrate encounters the barbarians he finds they are 'armed' without doubt, but armed in ways that are primitive: 'an ancient musket nearly as long as a man' (76). He counts 'three of the long-barrelled muskets; otherwise they bear short bows' (77).

The Magistrate's account undermines the Empire's assumptions about the dangers posed by the barbarians, for it reveals that these assumptions that then mushroom into invasive attacks launched by the Empire, are indeterminate, the product of a cultural fantasy. The Magistrate underscores the sexualized nature of this fantasy—the rape of daughters and wives—in his version and thus signals the repressive nature of prolonged boredom and leisure in the colonies.[3] But he categorizes the threat as a product of the Empire's imagination rather than founded on any empirical research into the barbarians. It is this set of rumours leading to categorization that eventually climaxes in the horrific scene of public flogging and branding 'ENEMY' (115, emphasis in original). Rumours of the barbarians, then, serve as an 'adhesive' and a catalyst for the Empire, enabling it to 'identify' the enemy and determining, forever, the relations between the colonials and the natives of the land. Thus rumours and unsubstantiated stories become *constitutive* of the violence between the so-called barbarians and the Empire.

Coetzee takes his title, and theme, from Constantine Cavafy's famous 'Waiting for the Barbarians'. Everybody awaits the barbarians: senators, the Emperor himself, consuls, distinguished orators and the townspeople. But by nightfall the barbarians have not turned up and the streets and squares start emptying. The speaker, worried, asks in the last lines:

> Now what's going to happen to us without barbarians?
> Those people were a kind of solution.
> (In Forché 491)

Rumours sustain the town because it is the rumour of barbarians arriving that enables everyday life to go on. Without the myth of invasion the town cannot survive, as both Cavafy and Coetzee suggest.

What rumour achieves in Coetzee's *Waiting for the Barbarians* is a resolution of the ambiguous and fluid situation of the border. The border here is the outpost of the Empire, with the imperium bordering so-called barbarian lands. The exact nature of the relations between the two is never defined, but what eventually resolves this ambiguous situation is the rumour of the barbarians' invasion of the Empire. Once this rumour is in place the ambiguity of the relations and situation is resolved because now the Empire knows how to proceed: it must attack the barbarians *first*.

This operation is put in place and Colonel Joll sends back prisoners. The Magistrate is shocked at the supposed threats to the Empire:

> Did no one tell him these are fishing people? It is a waste of time bringing them here! You are supposed to help him track down thieves, bandits, invaders of the Empire. Do these people look like a danger to the Empire? (18)

The rumour of barbarian invasion has effected an imperial invasion, the taking of prisoners and eventually the torture of those prisoners. It is in the rumour that the relations between the Empire and occupants of the lands are settled, so to speak. It is also the discursive construction of threat and enemy that climaxes in the denial of humane treatment and human rights of the prisoners.

But even before the tortures, another rumour ensures the dehumanization of the fisher-folk prisoners: 'a rumour begins to go the rounds that they are diseased, that they will bring an epidemic to the town' (21). Invasion by disease is the latest rumour. Coetzee suggests that there can be no Othering without *some* form of fugitive discourse about this Other.

In *Of Love and Shadows* the military establishment is angered, and threatened, by an innocuous pamphlet from Professor Leal. Signing the document 'Mikhail Bakunin' (the Russian anarchist), Professor Leal criticizes the military. In response the military issues a proclamation prohibiting 'public demonstration of any kind' and orders 'Citizen Bakunin [to] present himself voluntarily at the Ministry of Defense' (211–212). In Allende's satiric portrayal of the military, the latter is ignorant enough not to recognize the name 'Bakunin'. Bakunin in the military's ill-informed response is transformed into a citizen of *this* country. The establishment does not enquire into the reality of a 'Bakunin' and simply transforms the name into a symbol of local dissidence. The name 'Bakunin' becomes a way of framing the dissidents and identifying a source so that the event of the pamphlet might be interpreted. Bakunin becomes the explanation for dissidence, in the establishment's imaginary. The unsubstantiated and unproven *narrative source* of dissidence yet again enables the establishment's backlash against its own citizen, and thus serves as constitutive of ruler-citizen relations in the nation-state.

If in *Of Love and Shadows*, the establishment hears rumours of dissidence, in other cases, it is the citizenry of the nation-state that is hounded by rumours about imminent violence against specific groups of people. In *The Farming of Bones*, one cane-worker, Unèl, 'talk[s] about an order from the Generalissimo' (127) and Sebastien, another worker, responds to this with 'I don't know what to make of it … I keep hearing it, but I don't know if all of it is true' (127). Rumours accrete tension and panic through iteration here. The percentage of truth is open to question—'I don't know if all of it is true'—but the overall veracity, as Sebastien indicates, cannot be doubted. As a consequence, he is 'as troubled as the others' by what he hears (127).

In the same novel Amabelle the protagonist states a distrust of such stories:

> It couldn't be real. Rumors, I thought. There were always rumors, rumors of war, of land disputes, of one side of the island planning to invade the other. These were grand fantasies of presidents wanting the whole island to themselves. This could not touch people like me, nor people like Yves, Sebastien, and Kongo, who worked the cane fields. They were giving labor to the land. The Dominicans needed the sugar from the cane. (140)

Amabelle's thoughts appear here more in the form of a therapeutic discourse against the onslaught of rumours, and are equally fantastic. Her emphasis on the significance of labourers and their contribution to the island's economy is projected more as a slender belief that might or might not be proven right in the face of conflict. Thus, the narrative response to the rumours is also a mode of organizing social perceptions of the president, the Generalissimo and the public.

Rumours are deployed for an entirely different reason in Yasmina Khadra's *The Attack*. Sheikh Marwan, who is instrumental in organizing the resistance to the Israeli army, is never where he is. Dr Jaafari, the protagonist who is under Israeli scanners because his wife Sihem was a suicide bomber, seeks to meet Marwan to know of Sihem's true affiliations but is thwarted in his attempts. An acolyte informs Jaafari:

> Sheikh Marwan hasn't visited us here for ages. Rumors of his presence are spread to defend him from ambushes. Every time he wants to make an appearance somewhere, the word goes out that he's in Haifa, Bethlehem, Jenin, Gaza, Nuseirat, Ramallah, everywhere at the same time, in order to cover his tracks and protect his movements. The Israeli security forces are hot on his heels.(127)

Resistance, as Khadra demonstrates, also survives and indeed thrives, on rumour. Rumour here misleads, misidentifies and misdirects attention.

It possesses, as Bhabha noted, enormous performative power, and destabilizes the master/slave (in this case Israeli-Palestine) relations.

Rumours are modes of emplacement because they organize social perceptions of identities of both self and the Other in the HR text. They determine the social relations by offering frames of interpretation of events, even when these frames are suspect and the events themselves unclear. Having emplaced the self and the Other in antagonistic social relations the rumour prepares the ground for other forms of emplacement and identities.

Emplacement and the Moral Vacuum

'Without any particular relish, one of these men drew his sword and ran it through her.' This is Dave Eggers' Deng describing his viewing of a killing in *What is the What* (93). The utter indifference to the act, and the extinction of life, described in the minimalist prose embodies a key theme of HR literature: the absence of any emotional involvement/response or reflection leading to hesitation in brutal violence by the perpetrator.

HR literature throws up several examples of discursive constructions of humans where the perpetrators find distancing, legitimacy and justification for their cruelties. These anticipate the actual acts of torture and need to be read as preliminary and framing processes in which the HR subject is emplaced before being destroyed. For HR literature the dehumanization of individuals is made possible due to their emplacement in a condition of moral vacuums in systems and *discourses* of law and order, governance and social relations. This thematic of the moral vacuum as the source and place of dehumanization is illustrated in the interaction between torturer and tortured. Dehumanization is inflicted on the victim, but this does not leave the torturer unscathed. The destruction of the former's subjectivity alters the subject status of the torturer as well. The moral vacuum that HR literature examines gives considerable space, as a result, to structures that render some individuals helpless but also simultaneously dehumanize the victimizer even though they are not 'helpless' in the full sense of the word. To phrase it differently, HR literature is concerned with the emplacement of both victim *and* victimizer in moral vacuums, enabled by abstractions like the law, and which erodes all social relations irrevocably. The moral vacuum is the space of framing and apprehending of life in differential ways.

Herbert Kelman writes of the 'moral compact that governs human relationships' where humans perceive another as a human with agency and community (48–49). It demands that a human accept the individual 'as an end in himself, rather than a means toward some extraneous end' (49). Kelman makes the further point that 'those who participate in the massacre directly … are reinforced in their perception of the victim as less than human by observing their very victimization' (50). Thus, the victimizer loses the ability to empathize or care for the other, and this 'increases the dehumanization of the victimizer himself' (50–51). He loses, writes Kelman, 'both his sense of personal identity and his sense of community' (51). He simply obeys authority and implements routines. He chooses to not make judgements and choices that may be founded on his own values. In Kelman's words, 'he becomes alienated within his task' (51). He suffers from a 'psychic numbing'(52). Rowan Savage building on the work of Robert Jay Lifton proposes that the dehumanized 'discursive system regarding an out-group constitutes the (moral) reality within which members of the in-group act' (149). The perpetrator develops what Lifton termed the 'Auschwitz self' in which the meanings of one's actions were disavowed' (cited in Savage 149). While HR texts do not seek, in the main, to probe the psychology of the perpetrators (except in non-fictional accounts such as Jean Hatzfield's *Machete Season* (2005), based on conversations with the Hutu killers), they explore the emplacement of individuals within systems and discourses that enable the making of such an Auschwitz self.[4]

State systems that sanction certain types of killings create such spaces of moral vacuum, just as they approve mass-extermination modes like war. Specific ideologies, that very often redefine the human identities of potential victims, are put in place to provide the justification and legitimacy for extermination through dehumanization. The moral vacuum built into social relations as a consequence enables participation by people otherwise against killing humans. The 'cognitive dissonance' that may arise from participation in genocide (dissonance between the reluctance to take what is *visibly* a life and the participation in processes that take life) has to be quieted through dehumanization. Dehumanization, then, is a 'coherent narrative that allows one to justify one's actions to oneself as an individual, to all individuals within the perpetrator group, and to individual and collective bystanders and observers' (Savage 154).

The Magistrate in *Waiting for the Barbarians* sets out to examine this moral vacuum, this distance, made possible in the context of the Empire. His immediate emplacement in this moral vacuum, as victim to Joll and other tormentors, positions him suitably to probe the conditions under which the perpetrator(s) might lose their sense of the moral compact binding humans, their sense of personal identity and their sense of community when they begin to routinely torture, based on the orders issued by the authorities. On one occasion the Magistrate ponders about the moral vacuum in which the torturer is placed:

> I wonder how he felt the very first time: did he, invited as an apprentice to twist the pincers or turn the screw or whatever it is they do shudder even a little to know that at that instant he was trespassing into the forbidden? I find myself wondering too whether he has a private ritual of purification, carried out behind closed doors, to enable him to return and break bread with other men. Does he wash his hands very carefully, perhaps, or change all his clothes; or *has the Bureau created new men who can pass without disquiet between the unclean and the clean*? (13, emphasis added)

To the torturer Mandel the Magistrate addresses his puzzle:

> I am only trying to understand. I am trying to understand the zone in which you live. I am trying to imagine how you breathe and eat and live from day to day. But I cannot! (138)

He is unable to imagine, or read, Mandel's psyche, his everyday and his moral codes, admits the Magistrate. When the Empire classifies the nomads as (a) barbarians and (b) the Enemy, in its discourses it takes *difference* in identity and recategorizes this difference with a specific ideological twist as *threat*. Through this process anxieties and fears are projected onto the nomads and the Empire sets about eliminating them. The moral vacuum here, of course, is the negation of this nomad as a human in the eyes of Colonel Joll and his team. Violence shapes the interaction of Joll and the nomads because there is no longer a moral compact between the two (nomad and imperial individual or representative of the Empire). Johannes Lang, without using the term moral compact, addresses this collapse of interrelations: 'in place of intersubjective, even interpersonal exchanges, dehumanization leaves only a *void*' (228, emphasis added). This void is what I have called a moral vacuum. It generates, as James Waller has demonstrated in his painstaking study of ordinary Germans who participated in genocide (2002), a distance between victim and perpetrator, with no common ground.

HR literature metaphorizes the moral vacuum in particular ways, such as of reading, darkness and blindness or the inability to read/see. The inadequacy of cognitive knowledge represented in the trope of blinding or partial visibility is, I propose, a metaphor for the absence or loss of reflective and moral judgements. An emplacement in such a situation of cognitive and reflective-moral vacuum is central to the destruction of the subject in HR literature.

Hooding and blindfolding are common practices in torture and imprisonment (Eisenman 25–28, 107). HR texts frequently reference the blindfolding as a feature of this cognitive limitation placed upon both victim and perpetrator. This refusal to meet the eye of the victim, notes Dustin Byrd about war situations, was driven by a particular anxiety: 'how can one kill someone whom you see one's own reflection in?' (114). This anxiety resulted in training programmes in dehumanization where the 'humanity or sub-humanity of the other is not even considered', a process he calls 'nonhumanization' (114).

The descriptions of 'cold' eyes, expressionless faces and even, in cases such as *Requiem for a Woman's Soul*, of the torturers as they go about their 'activities' seem to suggest this 'void' (of Lang) in the social relations. In Alan Cumyn's *Man of Bone* Burridge finds the hood oppressive: 'I open my eyes but see only blackness ... the blackness is the hood' (7). In Dorfman's traumatic play, *Death and the Maiden*, Paulina is unable to testify against the torturers because she was always blindfolded while in jail and hence cannot identify them. In fact the play echoes the concluding parts of *Waiting for the Barbarians* in its extensive troping of partial visibility and darkness in order to capture the uncertainty around Paulina's sense of herself, of her former torturer and present existence. In the stage directions Paulina first appears illuminated only by the moonlight (89). When her husband enters the house, she hides in the darkness (89–90). When Paulina ties and gags Doctor Miranda it is illuminated by a dimmed moonlight, as 'a cloud passes over the moon' (103–104). In Patrícia Vieira's reading of this trope, she proposes: 'The blindfold, often used as a means to degrade prisoners, can simultaneously stand for their resistance to the unflinching eye of the oppressor' (132). However, I suggest that the absence of cognitive certainty for Paulina ensures that she utilizes her other senses to 'know' her perpetrator when he comes back in a different context:

> Blindfolded, yes. But I could still hear ... It's his voice. I recognised it as soon as he came in ... The way he laughs. Certain phrases he uses ... During all these years not an hour has passed that I haven't heard it, that same voice, next to me, next to my ear, that voice mixed with saliva, you think I'd forget a voice like his?' (107–108)

This means, Paulina operates through her other senses when the eyes fail, and the memory of her tormentor's smell and voice remains. Susana, captured and being transported in a van, records: 'it was dark; no light penetrated the hood I was wearing ... I seem to remember periods of light and darkness, night turning to day' (*Requiem for a Woman's Soul*, chapter III). Later too she describes how she 'lay hooded and motionless in the midst of a thick darkness' (chapter V).

Trying to look into Joll's or Mandel's eyes, the Magistrate sees—nothing. Susan Van Zanten Gallagher (1988) in her reading of these scenes of metaphoric blindness and blinding in Coetzee suggests that these are metaphors of the moral vacuum generated within the Empire. Joll wears dark glasses, and in the very opening paragraphs the Magistrate, struck by this feature, wonders: 'Is he blind?' (1). Later, the Magistrate meets the same, impenetrable, unreadable eyes in the torturer Mandel:

> I look into his clear blue eyes, as clear as if there were crystal lenses slipped over his eyeballs. He looks back at me. I have no idea what he sees. Thinking of him, I have said the word torture ... torturer to myself but they are strange words. (129)

Silas recognizes his torturer and his wife's rapist, Du Boise by his eyes in *Bitter Fruit* (9). In the ensuing conversation between Silas and Lydia, he remembers Du Boise's 'cold eyes' and the black sergeant's 'shame in his face' (14) and Lydia snaps: 'You don't remember my face, my tears' (14). It is the perpetrator's dehumanizing face and eyes that Silas remembers because he is struck by the moral vacuum that enabled Du Boise's act, cold, calculating and impervious to feeling. Susana records the 'small eyes and vicious stare' of her torturer El Rengo in *Requiem for a Woman's Soul* (chapter V). In *A Gesture Life* the doctor who is about to shoot Hata for defying him, 'had no malice or rage in his face, simply a plain expression of surprise' (270).

Empty eyes, unreadable eyes/faces and silences are metaphors for the moral vacuum that has permeated the perpetrator too. It marks the absence, or rather emptying, of cognition where the perpetrator now stops recognizing the victim as a human. The frames of cognition are disrupted, and consequently the perpetrator is able to perform his horrific actions with no disquiet over them or their consequences.

For instance, Doctor Karekazi, who is instrumental in one of the largest killings in *Murambi: The Book of Bones*, begins to see his marriage to a Tutsi woman as an error of judgement: 'I, having made a youthful mistake that destroyed my entire life, I will never forgive anyone again for spoiling our blood' ('Doctor Joseph Karekazi'). This is the moment when Karekazi has decided that his wife and children should also be killed with the rest of the Tutsis: 'I will not see them again' ('Doctor Joseph Karekazi'). Diop describes the moral vacuum in the 'butcher of Murambi' in terms of shadows and blurred outlines too:

> Tomorrow I will be there. Shadows in the dawn mist, facing the motionless trees. Screams will go upward toward the heavens. I will feel neither sadness nor remorse. There will be atrocious pain, of course, but only the weak hearted confuse crime with punishment ... I am not the kind of person who fears the shadows in his own soul.
> ('Doctor Joseph Karekazi')

The idiom of pure blood and organic purity that the Doctor deploys here functions as a mode of demonization: Tutsis and progeny born of relations with Tutsis are impure and could be exterminated for the purity of the Hutu nation (Straus 2001). The moral vacuum here—the absence of 'fear for the shadows in his soul', as the Doctor himself describes it—is the effect of the idiom of purity that eschews any human element outside that of the Hutu bloodline. By making the bloodline coterminous with the nation the Doctor effects a theory of immutable racial identity.

HR texts very often seek to unravel the emplacement of perpetrators in the moral vacuum of the system. Apartheid, totalitarianism and Empire 'created new men who can pass without disquiet between the unclean and the clean' as Coetzee puts it in *Waiting for the Barbarians*, and HR texts seek to understand such social and governance systems. This is metaphorized in HR literature as attempts to recognize, read and interpret secret and mystifying languages. HR texts therefore showcase processes of reading and interpretation as modes of unravelling the moral vacuum in which particular texts—such as torture—came to be written, legitimized and consumed. This is not the same as the occasion for and nature of storytelling by victims that are also components of HR literature, and to which I shall turn in a later chapter. Rather it is the theme of interpreting systemic moral vacuums that HR texts seem interested in because these emplace both victim and perpetrator.

Yet again, Coetzee offers us the key images that help us understand this necessity of analyzing emplacement. Coetzee's Magistrate seeks to understand the events that befell the blind girl, her feelings and her responses. The Magistrate who seeks to penetrate the silence of the tortured barbarian girl is, unconsciously, echoing the process of interrogation outlined by Colonel Joll:

> I am speaking of a situation in which I am probing for the truth, in which I have to exert pressure to find it. First I get lies, you see—this is what happens—first lies, then pressure, then more lies, then more pressure, then the break, then more pressure, then the truth. That is how you get the truth. (5)

Just as Joll seeks to reach the 'truth' through torture and incessant questioning, the Magistrate probes the girl's silences. Baffled at her continuing silence the Magistrate rants, 'what do I have to do to move you?' (47) This question in fact is that of a *torturer*, as the Magistrate recognizes in shock:

> With a shift of horror I behold the answer that has been waiting all the time to offer itself to me in the image of a face masked by two black glassy insect eyes from which comes no reciprocal gaze but only my doubled image cast back at me. (47)

He of course denies this recognition: 'No! No! No! I cry to myself ... There is nothing to link me with torturers, people who sit waiting like beetles in dark cellars ... I must assert my distance from Colonel Joll! (47).[5]

While one notes the Magistrate's horror at recognizing that he is emplaced in the same moral vacuum as Joll because he too had permitted tortures on the now-blind 'barbarian' girl, it is also important to note that Coetzee uses the infrahumanizing trope of animalization to describe torturers ('beetles'). The dark eyes of the Colonel, the beetles in the dark cellar resonate with the inability to see in the Magistrate and of course the blinded girl. Susan Gallagher proposes that the Magistrate finally recognizes his own complicity: 'Coetzee ... eliminate[es] the distinction between "them" and "us," the evil and the innocent' where 'everyone is guilty' (284). When the novel ends, Colonel Joll has lost the dark glasses, but Coetzee notes that the darkness at the heart of what he, and the Magistrate, represents, remains. As the Magistrate puts it: 'the crime that is latent in us we must inflict on ourselves … Not on others' (160). But the Colonel also has been infantilized in the process: 'he is no stronger than a child' (161). The Magistrate is also encased in the darkness. Coetzee uses darkness, invisibility and blurred sights in numerous combinations in this, the final encounter of Joll, the Magistrate and the ruins of Empire: 'blackness', 'faint blur', 'blue moonlight', 'blind … with splinters' (160), 'darkness', 'disappear into the night' (161) and 'darkness' (162). The Magistrate's fear of being blinded with splinters resonates with the tortures inflicted on the girl: 'They said they would burn her 'eyes out … The man brought the fork 'and made' her 'look at it. They held' her 'eyelids open', but she 'had nothing to tell them' (44).

Metaphors of darkness and shadows are indicative of morally ambiguous worlds in Dave Eggers' biographical novel, *What is the What* (O'Gorman 2015). Narrating the real-life story of Valentino Achak Deng in Sudan of the 1980s, it speaks of the 'Lost Boys', those displaced by the civil war in Sudan. The invaders of his village are 'like a shadow made by a low cloud … a shadow mov[ing] quickly over the land' (89). If this is a threatening shadow, others are refuge-spaces:

> I missed the shadow of my mother, listening to the sounds inside her. I had not realized how cold I had felt for so long. This woman gave me her shadow and I wanted to live within it until I could be home again. (264)

The Lost Boys occupy a 'shadow world' (269) and are themselves 'shadows' (156). The land itself, says Deng, was shadowed: 'a shadow grew over the land of my giraffes' (66). Eggers makes it clear that these are Lost Boys are mere shadows because they occupy a mediated zone where their lives have little or no value. This theme of low-value life is initiated early in the text when Deng's narrative addresses the readers:

> No doubt if you have heard of the Lost Boys of Sudan, you have heard of the lions. For a long while, the stories of our encounters with lions helped garner sympathy from our sponsors and adopted country in general. The lions enhanced the newspaper articles and no doubt played a part in the U.S being interested in us in the first place … As the hundreds of boys in my own group were walking through Sudan, five of us were taken by lions. (30)

These boys are shadows because they have been emplaced in two frames: the first of Sudanese civil war and its attendant crisis of living, the second the mediated attention of the world. Deng's comment above suggests that the boys exist in a zone between these two frames that evaluate them in particular ways. The first reduces them to expendable lives and the second evaluates them in terms of the lions that have devoured some of their companions. In the first frame the moral vacuum informs the heart of the Sudanese civil war where boys are hunted down and killed, or, if lucky, merely displaced from homes and families. In the second the moral vacuum informs the First World's consumption of boys-as-victims precisely because of the nature of embedded violence the trope of man-eating lions invokes. Deng points to the shallowness of global interest in the boys per se, clearly implying that the nature of decimation—being eaten by lions—is what drives media attention towards the survivors. Thus, the moral vacuum of reductionism in the Sudanese civil war is paralleled by the moral vacuum of global media interest in the exotic deaths of African boys. The boys escape the shadow world of the civil war to be emplaced in the discourse of 'exotic deaths' in the First World.

Infrahumanization, such as we will see in a later section, is possible because the *framing* of subjects and lives allows it to function. For instance, Hata the Korean who serves the Japanese army in Lee's *A Gesture Life* offers us a clear and concise account of the morally void system whose discursive construction—in military laws and norms—of the Other facilitates infrahumanization. Hata says:

> It was a matter of standards, in this case to apply the level of treatment that was most appropriate for the situation, and for whom. In this schema the commander had his level, the officers theirs, the enlisted men and others yet another, and so on and so forth, until it came to the girls, who had their own. All this was inviolable, like any set of natural laws. (226–227)

'Natural laws' in the military code of conduct enables the ill-treatment of comfort women and prisoners, as Hata notes. Even the murder of these women is not tantamount to homicide so that anybody who killed one of them would be 'charged not with murder, but with treasonous action against the corps ... as guilty as any saboteur who had stolen or despoiled the camp's armament or rations' (189). That a life might be taken in the same fashion as stealing arms or commodities suggests a moral vacuum that empowers the taking of the life. K, the Korean comfort girl Hata hopes to marry, points out that she is just a sexual commodity, framed in that manner by the masculine ethos of the military but also due to the national identities that reinforced in the course of the war. She says: 'I will tell you now, it is my sex. The thing of my sex. If you could cut it from me and keep it with you like a pelt or favorite stone, that would be all' (300). Captain Ono also undermines Hata's faith in her presumed chastity when, in the course of mocking Hata, Ono says:

> I'm letting the pregnancy go, in fact, to see how long she'll stay that way, once she begins servicing the whole of the camp. She was pregnant before even I was able to take my pleasure. Before anyone here had her. Who knows who her real master is? The commander and I certainly aren't. (270)

K is pointing to the absence of a moral code that treats the women as humans and not objects of sexual gratification alone. Ono while appearing to suggest K's sexual agency (marked as promiscuity) chooses to ignore the circumstances in which K is placed.[6] After her brutal rape and cannibalistic murder by over thirty soldiers, Hata goes to find her body. The account runs thus:

> I could not smell, or hear, or see as I did my medics work. I could not feel my hands as they gathered, nor could I feel the weight of such remains. And I could not sense that other, tiny, elfin form I eventually discovered, miraculously whole, I could not see the figured legs and feet, the utter blessed digitisation of the hands. Nor could I see the face, the perfected cheek and brow. Its pristine sleep still unbroken, undisturbed. And I could not know what I was doing, or remember any part. (305)

Alexis Motuz reads this scene as a trauma narrative:

> Hata's recollection reveals that, at the moment of its occurrence, the discovery of K's body registers as non-experience, and therefore, he cannot undergo the process of abreaction in which the affect attached to memory wears away. (2013: 415)

While Lee's account does approximate to a trauma narrative, the loss of senses and cognitive dislocation recalls the metaphors of shadows on shadows, darkness, invisibility/partial visibility in Coetzee, Dangor, Rivabella and Eggers' texts dealing with the moral vacuum. It is this blindness and moral vacuum that allows such a framing of life and inflicting of brutality upon that life.

Expropriation and the New Social Order

In *What is the What* Deng's father pleads with the rebel militia:

> I can give you some sugar, of course … I remember the struggle. I know the struggle needs to be fed … But I can't give you the entire bag. That would cripple my business … I'll give you as much as I can.(67)

The soldier, furious, responds: 'We'll take this bag and you'll be grateful we don't take more' (67). For protesting, Deng's father is kicked in the face in full view of the village because the soldiers needed to make an example of his humiliation (68). The insult is not merely corporeal: it is the expropriation of the man's store, his business and his livelihood all of which have suddenly become the property of somebody else. The act radically redefines forever the social relations of Marial Bal where the Dengs live. The act of expropriation is a crucial one, as Deng records soon after describing this incident: 'And that day, the rebel presence was established and Marial Bal became a town at war with itself' (68).

The logical next step after dehumanization and infrahumanization as thematized in HR literature is expropriation. The seizure of property and identities, of life itself, of victims becomes the hallmark of the genocidal imaginary because, having demonized the Other, it becomes imperative to deny them the right to all forms of property, including the property of their own names or bodies. The 'routine degradations that fall within the categories of social and economic rights' might be read as 'signs and warnings that the ultimate atrocity [genocide] is imminent' (Goldberg 2007: 153). Expropriations *are* these signs.

In Lorne Shirnian's play about the Armenian genocide, *Exile in the Cradle*, the first moves, besides asking Armenians for their identification papers, from the Turkish government are expropriative ones. Hagop tells the young soldier, Salim, who has accosted him for papers:

'I am a wealthy man … And the soldier cuts his speech short with: 'no longer. All Armenian financial assets in Ottoman banks have been seized.' (36)

Expropriation in the HR text is the socio-economic accompaniment to endo-colonialism's genocidal imaginary. In each of these texts, the seizure of property is prelude and preliminary to the seizure and destruction of life-as-property. Expropriation rejects the rule of law, to begin with, and erases norms of socially acceptable behaviour. When, for instance, the old shopkeeper is abused and his property taken from him, without payment, in *What is the What*, the very institution of the marketplace has been destroyed. But, as the militia point out, this destruction is metonymic for the loss of life itself. The claiming of Armenian property and wealth for the Turkish nation in Shirnian's play marks the redefinition of public policy itself. The large-scale participation of soldiers and militia in such actions constitutes the social upheaval that precedes or accompanies genocides.

Thus, it seems to come as no surprise in *What is the What* that after the militia raid and take away material from stores, they turn their attention to the girls in Deng's village, several of whom are taken away as commodities: 'they threw each girl onto a saddle and then used rope to secure them, as they would a rug or a bundle of kindling' (93). Almost coterminous with the massacres are the expropriations of property—such as cattle and horses (101).[7] In Jane Harrison's *Stolen*, a play about the 'Stolen Generation'—where Aboriginal children were forcibly taken away from their parents and families and given foster homes by the state, 1860s–1930s—the expropriation is justified in terms of the responsibility towards the children in dysfunctional (indigenous) families. Expropriation of boys and girls during Argentina's Dirty War (1976–1979) is also now part of the historical record.

Demonization

> 'No screaming here! No bitching! Hear me? Now fill out the forms, you dirty little leftist'
>
> 'But I'm not-'
>
> 'Shut your mouth and write!'

This is the first interaction-interrogation in the prison for the protagonist of Farnoosh Moshiri's *The Bathhouse* (20–21). In Ariel Dorfman's *Widows*, the Captain confronted with the Fuentes family declares 'suspected subversives will be interrogated according to official procedures' (45). Burridge is 'identified' as a Central Investigation Agency (CIA) operative and incarcerated in *Man of Bone*. During his torture he is abused and mocked as a CIA man (20).Susana in Omar Rivabella's *Requiem for a Woman's Soul* is simply a 'seditious pig' (chapter III) and elsewhere a 'seditious little whore' (chapter V). In Allende's *Of Love and Shadows* potential threats are from 'Marxists'.

In all four cases there is no individual any longer: the prison has incarcerated a type, and a type that is supposedly a functioning *threat*. Dehumanization here works as a mode of demonizing the Other. By reducing the individual to a type, or a group identity, dehumanization as an act of 'collective framing' (Hagan and Rymond-Richmond 2008: 876) works in ways that render the individual into one-dimensional sources of threats. The leftist, the CIA operative, the communist are conceptualizations rather than individuals in these texts. Dustin Byrd describes this mode of dehumanization as processing a 'concept with life' (108) in order to elicit hostility.

Dehumanization here is a process of demonization. Demonization is a form of subject-destroying identification that is in itself an act of power, because one party possesses the power to identify some-other in this manner. I argue, after Byrd, that this dehumanization-as-demonization has a two-step movement. One, it collapses all singularity into a generality: the individual is only a type. Second, it conceptualizes the type itself as non-identity. This means, the 'communist', the 'leftist' or the 'seditious' were experienced as the category that did not fit within the identity of whatever identity the country's powers had decided it had to be. That is, the characterization and conceptualization of individuals as seditious, radicals, dissenters or communists was a way of saying that these were identities that did not fit within the country's definitions of itself, and therefore were 'other', 'foreign' or 'not-us'. Such identities cannot be an organic component of the country which had defined itself differently. For example, Moshiri's *The Bathhouse* shows how Iran had defined itself almost entirely as an Islamic state given to the adoration of the country's holy leader. Part of the justification for the imprisonment and torture of 'nonbelievers' was: they could not see the 'Sacred Face of the Great Leader on the moon' (9). Iranians, in this definition, would and could see the Sacred Face, and those who did not were seditious, traitorous and anti-national.

In this form of dehumanization the bestowing of the identity as 'seditious' or 'leftist' not only rendered the individual into a non-identity: it demonized them into a threat.[8] Since this form of dehumanization mostly targets, in HR literature, *citizens* of a nation, it causes a state to turn against its own people and looks for enemies within its borders. Dehumanization is a response to the perceived auto-immune disorder represented by the citizenry in these novels, and enables the discourse to present the nonconformists as threats to be neutralized. It then becomes imperative that the state embark on a process of self-defence against such threats. Given the threats from within the nation, it becomes imperative, says the rhetoric of the state, to defend and cleanse the country. Faustin Gasana in *Murambi*, one of the Hutu killers, says: 'I know that the Tutsis and us, we could never live together. Never.' He thereby denies, or rejects, the history of coexistence, transforming the relations between the two into one of irreducible and irrefutable antagonism. Within the same country, in Gasana's belief, the Tutsis are collectively framed as Other.[9]

Says the Captain in Dorfman's *Widows*:

> It sickens me, I hate pain, terror, but at times I'm forced to … We have to follow our hearts to the greater good. There are forces at work here—who intend nothing good for this country. Intend peace … But sometimes the road to peace is, as you know, fraught with difficult choices. (42)

After listening to the Magistrate speak extensively on the injustice and ridiculousness of waging war on the poverty-stricken 'barbarians' in Coetzee's *Waiting for the Barbarians*, Colonel Joll loses his temper and yells: 'You are simply ignorant of the facts. You are living in a world of the past. You think we are dealing with small groups of peaceful nomads. In fact we are dealing with a well organized enemy.' To this the Magistrate retorts: 'those pitiable prisoners you brought in—are *they* the enemy I must fear?'(125, emphasis in original).The prison warden in *The Bathhouse* lectures the prisoners on the state: 'Our Leader is chosen by Allah and our government is the government of Allah. Come to the other side of the pool and sit in the ranks of the devotees' (52).

The citizens here are 'devotees', and politically enfranchised individuals later. The Captain in *Widows*, the Hutu militia in *Murambi*, the soldiers in *Of Love and Shadows*, the prison wardens in *The Bathhouse* become defenders of the nation-state and its one true ideology. In contrast with the dehumanized Other, they project themselves in their genocidal imaginary as guardians. In fact, Gasana the Hutu killer, experiences a 'sensation' of warrior-dom: 'I have the sensation of reliving a scene from ancient times, from times when the bravery of warriors was exalted before battle' (*Murambi*, 'Faustin Gasana').

The imprisoned in *The Bathhouse* are those whose devotion is suspect, and therefore their categorization is radically different, as we see in the next sentence: 'Bring them here. Let these devils learn their lesson tonight' (52). After the women are flogged, they repent and concede that they do see the Sacred Face on the moon, the warden announces: 'From this moment on you are a repentant. Wear this hood and serve the Holy Republic' (54). The prison and the attendant punishments are intended to reform the inhuman into full-fledged citizens, whose identities would then fit that which the state has decided will be the official one. 'Pig', 'barbarian' and other designations in these texts demote the individual to a non-human entity but simultaneously assign these ' "life-like" creature[s] with negative attributes, which transform them into a threat' (Byrd 105). Barbarians, nonbelievers, communists and leftists are *identities* first and human persons later: identities that represent threats to the nation-state's definitions of itself and therefore must either be reformed or eliminated.

In each of these novels the destruction of subjectivity is seen as a legitimate process conducted by the state in order to protect itself from its enemies *within*. Having set in place a discourse of 'internal externality'—internal in the sense of geographical and social coexistence but external in fundamental psychological terms—the state empowers the disappearance of its own citizenry as a mode of protecting the homogenous, standardized idea of the nation (Kallis 2002: 28). The cultural imagery of one faith, one ideology and one ideal—peace, Islam, socialism or development in the novels cited above—enables the state to mark the Cecilias (*Imagining Argentina*), the Susanas (*Requiem for a Woman's Soul*), the Irenes (*Of Love and Shadows*), the Partnoys (*The Little School*) as internal externalities who need to be erased to enable the march of the state. This sense of internal threat is voiced by the sergeant in Allende's *Of Love and Shadows*:

> Do you know what would happen the minute the General fell from power, God forbid? The Marxists would rise up and slit the throats of every soldier, along with their wives and children. (245)

This march of the state over the internal externalities demands dehumanization. The legitimization is possible only if the first stage, dehumanization, has been put in place through mechanisms such as the law. Endo-colonialism is a process of emplacement where individuals are put into categories that are perceived as threats to the nation.[10] These categories function as cultural symbols that are then omniscient, persuasive and hate-inducing.

Endo-colonialism is another name for systemic violence in HR literature. Purges, rapes, disappearances, mass incarcerations and executions are the norm in such societies in *Imagining Argentina, A Gesture Life, Of Love and Shadows, The Bathhouse, What is the What, Widows* and other texts. Endo-colonialism operates also in socio-economic modes in terms of housing, healthcare and employment. Once dehumanization is accepted as a normative state of affairs in any society, HR literature shows, the individual's emplacement within it renders her/him a victim.

The state in such HR texts pursues its goals, irrespective of the effects it has on social relations and the lives of citizens. It is important to note that in HR literature, then, systemic violence does not revolve around individual events but manifests as 'normative violence that operates within the system's routine functioning' (Byrd 119). For instance, raids on journalists and search operations are common occurrences in the lives of people in *Of Love and Shadows.* Neighbours suspect each other, spy on each other and betray each other. Patients betray their physicians in *The Bathhouse*, so as to ingratiate themselves with the state. Spies insinuate themselves into crowds in order to locate 'subversives' in *Imagining Argentina.* Systemic violence here translates into increasing instances of eroding social relations in which the individuals are emplaced.

Infrahumanization

Vijila in 'The Autobiography of a Bitch' describes the Dalits, of which she is one, as infrahumans to the upper castes:

> In their markets
> We've neither milk, flesh
> Nor skin.
> We're not offerings
> For their gods either.
> (Vijila 2012: 40)

In Diop's *Murambi* the term 'cockroaches', as a descriptor used by Hutus about the Tutsis, occurs throughout the text. Faustin Gasana, one of the Hutu killers in *Murambi* through whose narrative part of the story is told, says of his old and dying father: 'I have never heard him pronounce the word "Tutsi." He always calls them "them" or "Inyenzi," literally cockroaches' (*Murambi*, 'Faustin Gasana'). In Erik Ehn's play about Rwanda's genocide, *Maria Kizito*, as in Murambi, the term is used as a descriptor for Tutsis (191). 'Pig' is a descriptor in *Requiem for a Woman's Soul.* The Magistrate in *Waiting for the Barbarians* protests at

Colonel Joll preparing to beat him and others with a hammer, screaming: 'You would not use a hammer on a beast, not on a beast!' (117). Indeed this animalizing has been anticipated in Colonel Joll's hunting expedition. He declares to the Magistrate: 'thousands of deer, pigs, bears were slain, so many that a mountain of carcasses had to be left to rot' (1). The Lieutenant tells the Captain in Dorfman's *Widows*: 'These people are used to being beaten ... make sure they don't forget who's holding the leash. If you are holding the leash' (53). In *Of Love and Shadows*, when stopped by a patrol, Francisco is abused as a 'faggot' (122). In Dorfman's *Death and the Maiden* the women inmates are 'bitches' (136).

In Dalit poetry from India, we see other instances of such an infrahumanization. In Vincent Raj's 'Clutching the End of My Saree' (2013), an impoverished mother seeking work is followed by her children, who then become ear-witnesses to the abuse the local policeman flings her way:

> "Slut! Hot as ever, aren't you?"
> The taunts of the police
> I feel I am dead.
> (Raj 2012: 23)

It is the abuse that reduces her to nothing, so that the 'I feel I am dead' reflects less a state of death than the death of feelings, an emptying of affective subjectivity. A certain form of gendered infrahumanization is the subject of numerous such poems from India. In Kalesh's *Hairpin Bend*, the Dalit girl who goes out to work is described thus by the speaker:

> On the way even if anyone comments
> On the growing heaviness of her tiny breasts
> And the fine down on her limbs...
> She says nothing
> (Kalesh 2012: 43–44)

In the poem the young girl's body is the site of labour and social opprobrium for performing this same life-sustaining labour. It is a body emplaced at the intersection of the financial and cultural economy—between labour-for-wage and verbal abuse or social opprobrium (Nayar 2015).

Racial and animal epithets, and cursing are integral to the process of 'genocidal priming' (Hinton, cited in Hagan and Rymond-Richmond 881). Curses enable a degrading transformation.

> Curses draw on the communal language and its primordial sensibility about the relationship between the sacred and the profane … Cursing sets up violence to be a sacrifice to honor the attacker as a priest representing the collective moral being. (Katz 1988, cited in Hagan and Rymond-Richmond 2008: 882)

In infrahumanization the human individual is reduced to a subhuman or animal status. When the potential victims are emplaced in situations of structural helplessness, such as in the days leading up to genocide (*Murambi*) or while in custody (*Death and the Maiden*, *Waiting for the Barbarians*), infrahumanization redefines the social relations between murderers/wardens/torturers and victims. Thus, infrahumanization is a mode of *social distancing* wherein perpetrators escape the moral dilemmas, if any, of participating in the killing or torture of human beings. I am not looking at the debasement of embodied subjectivity through the *practice* of torture as much as the *discourses* of infrahumanization that lead up to and frame the possibilities of torture itself.

Animal imagery such as the above becomes essential because grafting a new identity—leftist, communist, subversive—was not adequate to entirely de-individualize the individual. Johannes Lang writes: 'Stripping the deportees of their civilian appearance deprived them of the outward signs of their individual identities, but it did not in any straightforward sense undermine their humanity', just as 'attributing a host of generalized negative characteristics … essentialized them by subordinating their individual complexities to collective descriptions' without reducing them to the non-human (234). Infrahumanization in the form of animalization tropes ensures that the perpetrators no longer *see* the individual victims as moral beings or subjects. It denies the individual agency and autonomy because animals might be controlled or even killed with impunity. The Magistrate in *Waiting for the Barbarians* comes to recognize this infrahumanization, this ultimate abjection, of himself after the tortures inflicted on him: 'there is no way of dying allowed me, it seems, except of a dog in a corner' (128).

In *Requiem for a Woman's Soul* Susana is raped repeatedly and brutally. In *Bitter Fruit* Lydia is raped by the white policeman in Apartheid South Africa. Cecilia and her daughter Teresa, a minor, are meted the same treatment in *Imagining Argentina*. Susana and Teresa are eventually killed. Cecilia and Lydia survive, but expectedly broken in body and spirit. In these texts infrahumanization acquires a new dimension. Rape, as Lang notes, does not deny the victim subjectivity—in fact the power of rape hinges on the acknowledgement of the victim's subjective suffering (236). But, as Lang notes in the case of murders following rape, the 'rape is committed against a human being, but once it has been carried out the perpetrators availed themselves of dehumanizing images in order to trivialize the act's moral consequences' (236).[11] This latter is achieved by then calling the woman by animal names—'bitches' in Dorfman's *Death of a Maiden* or in Rivabella's *Requiem for a Woman's Soul* (XIII), for example. The comfort women in Chang-rae Lee's *A Gesture Life* are referred to in derogatory terms. Hata, Lee's protagonist finds the 'casualness' of the Japanese soldier's usage, 'as if he were speaking of any animal in a pen' objectionable for, as he notes, he 'certainly did not think of the other girls as animals' (250–251). But he admits that they were only 'parts of the larger mechanism of his living, the steady machine that grinds along each night and day' (251).

Infrahumanization here is the combination of two specific moves: the retention of the victim as a fully conscious subject whose subjectivity is corrosively destroyed, and the dehumanization into an animal so she can then be slaughtered after sex or rape. In Coetzee's *Disgrace*, in a particular horrific imagining, Lurie imagines the rape of his daughter Lucy. The entire sequence is cast in infrahumanizing terms:

> the men, for their part, drank up her fear, revelled in it, did all they could to hurt her, to menace her, to heighten her terror. *Call your dogs!* They said to her. *Go on call your dogs! No dogs? Then let us show you dogs!*
>
> He can, if he concentrates, if he loses himself, be there, be the men, inhabit them, fill them with the ghost of himself. *The question is, does he have it in him to be the woman.* (160, emphasis in original)

Lucy Graham has argued that in this scene 'Lurie's question suggests that ethical responsiveness depends on experiencing the narrative differently—not from the viewpoint of perpetrator or voyeur, but from the position of weakness and suffering' (2003: 444). Graham's attention is focused on how Lurie views Lucy's rape, and misses the infrahumanization implicit in the language Lurie *imagines* was used by the rapists. Lurie imagines himself in the same role as the rapists, where he would become the animal they had been in the course of their assault on her. In the act of violence, both victim and perpetrator, suggests Coetzee, occupy the same plane: as animals. The act of rape, as Coetzee frames it, is enabled and framed within a *discourse* of infrahumanization. Incidentally, Lucy is left alive after her rape, and she sees herself as dead. In a note to her father, David Lurie, she writes: 'I am a dead person and I do not know yet what will bring me back to life' (161). The Magistrate in *Waiting for the Barbarians* sees himself being transformed into a beast or a 'simple machine' (93), the latter signifying automata rather than organic life.

Gérard Nayinzira in *Murambi* survives the massacre through a process wherein he performs a self-infrahumanization. Boubacar Diop offers us the account from Nayinzira's perspective:

> I allowed myself to be covered by the bodies of the first victims. But I was still half visible. So I prayed really hard for others to fall next to me and that's what happened. I had blood on my clothes, in my eyes, everywhere ... I was obliged to swallow and then spit out their blood, it went into my whole body ... I kept splashing around in their blood. ('Murambi')

In the enforced mixing of blood from the dead and dying, life continues for and in Nayinzira. It is the structural helplessness of the Tutsis that Diop highlights here in order to focus our attention on the processes through which those considered cockroaches—infrahumanization in the genocidal discourse of the Hutus—and of impure bloodline survive. Infrahumanization is the breaking of a taboo, as Nayinzira cannibalizes the dead in order to live.

***

In the catalogue of individuals disappeared through dehumanization, persons become statistics, thus adding to their dehumanized states. Writes Allende in *Of Love and Shadows*:

> They [families of the disappeared] went from place to place, asking futile questions, and received nothing but the advice to consider the men dead ... Papers were lost in offices, and with the passing of time they saw their hopes fading like the lines of an old drawing. (253)

Imagining Argentina seeks to recuperate them by having Carlos tell their stories, especially of their last moments so that their families and friends have some sense of how their loved ones died. Michael Ondaatje offers a very short inventory of the dead as part of *Anil's Ghost*, but offers us an additional slice of information: the last sightings of the disappeared individuals:

> *Kumara Wijetunga, 17. 6th November 1989. At about 11.30 p.m. from his house.*
> *Prabath Kumara, 16. 17th November 1989. At 3.20 a.m. from the home of a friend...*
> *Manelka da Silva, 17. 1st December 1989. While playing cricket...*
> *Weeratunga Samaraweera, 30. 7th January 1990. At 5.00 p.m. while going for a bath at Hulandawa Panamura.*
>
> (41, emphases in original)

This is printed on an unnumbered page in the Picador edition, adding to the poignancy of the statistical dehumanization of the disappeared. Victoria Burrows interprets the enigmatic inventory to mean an 'unlocated, depersonalized testimony' (2008: 170–171). At one level it is indeed a depersonalized listing of random disappeared persons. But at another level, it also serves as powerful symbolism where the numbers who disappeared are in fact *persons*. It is in their disappearances from their everyday life, wearing specific clothing, performing specific and routine actions or from particular locations, for instance, that we *see* the subject who has disappeared.

Emplacement in HR literature is a study of the contexts, liveable or unliveable, of life itself. From rumours to infrahumanization, worlds are unmade so that life is unliveable and subjectivities unsustainable. Emplacement plays a key role in the making of the genocidal imaginary which is the anterior moment to the violation of subjects and subject-worlds. It is thus a frame or an outwork, in the examination of the subject of Human Rights. Since all ontology is social ontology, HR literature opens with the socius in which all subjectivity is located. From this it moves inwards, and studies the corporeality of the subject of HR, as we shall now see.

Notes

1. The term 'genocide' itself, since its coinage by Raphael Lemkin, has been debated and redefined almost continuously. In addition to the UN's definition, we have among the most commonly used ones, Helen Fein's: 'Genocide is sustained purposeful action by a perpetrator to physically destroy a collectivity directly or indirectly, through interdiction of the biological and social reproduction of group members, sustained regardless of the surrender or lack of threat offered by the victim' (1993). And I.W. Charny's: 'genocide in the generic sense is the mass killing of substantial numbers of human beings, when not in the course of military action

against the military forces of an avowed enemy, under conditions of the essential defenselessness and helplessness of the victims' (1994). See David Moshman (2001) for a summary.

2. Haitian immigrant workers in the Dominican Republic were massacred in 1937 by Generalissimo Rafael Trujillo. The protagonist of the tale is Amabelle Desir, born in Haiti but raised in the Dominican Republic by Dominicans after the death of her parents by drowning. After the massacre Amabelle goes to Haiti.
3. See Saikat Majumdar on boredom in the colonial imagination (2013).
4. Instances of individuals who, when emplaced within particular systems of thought and beliefs, are encouraged and empowered to perform genocidal actions, have been documented in studies of Nazi officers. See David Goldhagen's *Hitler's Willing Executioners* (1997). Goldhagen states early in his text that it is not merely the 'incentive structure' in which the perpetrators operate that produce such actions but 'the incentive structure … in conjunction with the cognitive and value structures' together that produce the actions (21). Other accounts of such emplacement of perpetrators may be found in Rudolph Höss' *Death Dealer: The Memoirs of the SS Kommandant at Auschwitz* (1996) and Christopher Browning's *Ordinary Men* (1992).
5. Rosemary Jolly writes about the Magistrate's attempts as resonant of Joll's: there is one aspect of his 'reading' of the barbarian 'girl' that corresponds to Joll's 'writing' and 'reading' of her. By making her body into a sign that becomes the figure of the truth, both Joll and the magistrate turn the 'girl' into an other whose person, outside of that figuring, is irrelevant to them. (cited in Nashef 2010: 24)
6. K, writes Young-Oak Lee, was 'victimized under patriarchal colonialism, in which he [Hata] also was complicit. Mourning the death of his national self and the death of humanity, he cannot construct his identity in a nation that condones brutality' (2005: 152).
7. One notes that the 'disappearing' by expropriation, especially of girls, continues as a strategy in conflict, most recently exemplified by the 2014 kidnap of 300 plus girls by Boko Haram in Sudan.
8. I revise this in the wake of the students of India's prestigious Jawaharlal Nehru University, New Delhi, being charged with sedition, February 2016.
9. Lee Ann Fujii notes:
   The story that the *génocidaires* told was grounded in long-accepted historical "truths" that Rwandan schoolchildren learned in school, to wit: Tutsi were foreign invaders from Ethiopia who had stolen Rwanda from its rightful inhabitants; as Hamites, they shared no natural kinship with the Hutu majority who were of Bantu origin and were therefore the Hutu's "natural enemy". (2004: 102)

10. Ironically, if they have been 'disappeared' as subversives, as is the case with Cecilia in *Imagining Argentina*, they are simultaneously 'off the record'. General Guzman, upon Carlos' inquiry as to his missing wife (Cecilia) informs him: 'Their names are not on the list so they have not committed any crimes. If you do not know where they are it is because some leftist group has taken them to make us look bad. We do nothing to innocent people' (107). Having been picked up for being a subversive and disappeared, Cecilia now joins the ranks of the missing innocents.
11. Commentators have suggested that rape might be considered integral to warfare. Beverley Allen termed it 'rape warfare' and 'genocidal rape' in her study of Bosnia. Darfur and Rwanda were genocides wherein the rape of racially and ethnically different was organized systematically: Darfur had rape camps and Tutsi women were systematically raped by soldiers with AIDS to enforce pregnancy (see Allen 1996 and Card 2008).

Bibliography

Allen, Beverley. 1996. *Rape Warfare: The Hidden Genocide in Bosnia-Herzegovina and Croatia*. Minneapolis: University of Minnesota Press.

Barman, Manoranjan. 2012. Shabori. In *Survival and Other Stories: Bangla Dalit Fiction in Translation*, trans. Siddhartha Biswas and eds. Sankar Prasad Singha and Indranil Acharya, 105–112. Hyderabad: Orient BlackSwan.

Bhabha, Homi K. [1994] 2009. By Bread Alone: Signs of Violence in the Mid-nineteenth Century. In *The Location of Culture*. 283–302. London: Routledge.

Browning, Christopher R. [1992] 2001. *Ordinary Men: Reserve Police Battalion 101 and the Final Solution in Poland*. New York: Penguin.

Burrows, Victoria. 2008. The Heterotopic Spaces of Postcolonial Trauma in Michael Ondaatje's *Anil's Ghost*. *Studies in the Novel* 40(1–2): 161–177.

———. 2009. *Frames of War: When is Life Grievable?* London: Verso.

Byrd, Dustin. 2013. Neither Man Nor Beast: Dehumanization in Direct and Systemic Violence. *memoria ethnologica* nr. 48–49. An XIII: 105–118.

Card, Claudia. 2008. The Paradox of Genocidal Rape Aimed at Enforced Pregnancy. *Southern Journal of Philosophy* 46(S1): 176–189.

Charny, I.W. 1994. Toward a Generic Definition of Genocide. In *Genocide: Conceptual and Historical Dimensions*, ed. G.J. Andreopoulos. Philadelphia: University of Pennsylvania Press.

Derby, Lauren. 2014. Beyond Fugitive Speech: Rumor and Affect in Caribbean History. *Small Axe* 18(2): 123–140.

Espeland, Rune Hjalmar. 2011. Autochthony, Rumor Dynamics, and Communal Violence in Western Uganda. *Social Analysis* 55(3): 18–34.

Fein, Helen. 1993. *Genocide: A Sociological Perspective*. New York: Sage.

Forché, Carolyn. 1993. Ed. *Against Forgetting: The Poetry of Witnessing*. New York: WW Norton.

Fujii, Lee Ann. 2004. Transforming the Moral Landscape: The Diffusion of a Genocidal Norm in Rwanda. *Journal of Genocide Research* 6(1): 99–114.

Gallagher, Susan Van Zanten. 1988. Torture and the Novel. JM Coetzee's *Waiting for the Barbarians. Contemporary Literature* 29(2): 277–285.

Goldberg, Elizabeth Swanson. 2007. *Beyond Terror: Gender, Narrative, Human Rights*. New Brunswick: Rutgers University Press.

Goldhagen, Daniel Jonah. 1997. *Hitler's Willing Executioners: Ordinary Germans and the Holocaust*. New York: Vintage.

Graham, Lucy Valerie. 2003. Reading the Unspeakable: Rape in J.M. Coetzee's *Disgrace. Journal of Southern African Studies* 29: 433–444.

Haagensen, Lisa, and Marnix Croes. 2012. Thy Brother's Keeper? The Relationship Between Social Distance and Intensity of Dehumanization During Genocide. *Genocide Studies and Prevention* 7(2–3): 223–250.

Hagan, John, and Wenona Rymond-Richmond. 2008. The Collective Dynamics of Racial Dehumanization and Genocidal Victimization in Darfur. *American Sociological Review* 73: 875–902.

Hatzfield, Jean. 2005. *Machete Season*. Trans. Linda Coverdale. New York: Farrar, Straus and Giroux.

Höss, Rudolf. 1996. *Death Dealer: The Memoirs of the SS Kommandant at Auschwitz*. Ed. Steven Paskuly. Trans. Andrew Pollinger. Boston: De Capo Press.

Kalesh, S. 2012. Hairpin Bend. In *The Oxford Anthology of Malayalam Dalit Writing*, trans. Sreekumar Varma and eds. M.V. Dasan, V. Prathiba, Pradeepan Pampkirikunnu, and C.S. Chandrika, 43–44. New Delhi: Oxford University Press.

Kallis, Aristotle. 2002. *Genocide and Fascism: The Eliminationist Drive in Eastern Europe*. New York: Routledge.

Kelman, Herbert C. 1973. Violence Without Moral Restraint: Reflections on the Dehumanization of Victims and Victimizers. *Journal of Social Issues* 29(4): 25–61.

Lang, Johannes. 2010. Questioning Dehumanization: Intersubjective Dimensions of Violence in the Nazi Concentration and Death Camps. *Holocaust and Genocide Studies* 24(2): 225–246.

Langlois, Anthony J. 2005. The Narrative Metaphysics of Human Rights. *International Journal of Human Rights* 9(3): 369–387.

Lee, Young-Oak. 2005. Gender, Race, and the Nation in *A Gesture Life. Critique* 46(2): 146–159.

Majumdar, Saikat. 2013. *Prose of the World: Modernism and the Banality of Empire*. New York: Columbia University Press.

Moshman, David. 2001. Conceptual Constraints on Thinking About Genocide. *Journal of Genocide Research* 3(3): 431–450.

Motuz, Alexis. 2013. Before Speech: An Interrogation of Trauma in Chang-Rae Lee's *A Gesture Life*. *Canadian Review of American Studies* 43(3): 411–432.

Moulin, Caroline. 2010. Border Languages: Rumors and (Dis)Placements of (Inter)National Politics. *Alternatives* 35: 347–371.

Nashef, Hania A.M. 2010. Becomings in J. M. Coetzee's *Waiting for the Barbarians* and José Saramago's *Blindness*. *Comparative Literature Studies* 47(1): 21–41.

Nayar, Pramod K. 2015. Dalit Poetry and the Aesthetics of Traumatic Materialism. *Indian Journal of Gender Studies* 22(1): 1–14.

O'Gorman, Daniel. 2015. [N]ew Constellations for Thinking About Normativity: Rethinking Judith Butler's 'Frame' with Reference to Dave Eggers' *What is the What*. *Textual Practice* 29(4): 653–674.

Raj, A. Vincent. 2012. Clutching the End of My Saree. In *The Oxford Anthology of Tamil Dalit Poetry*, trans. Ravi Shankar and eds. Ravikumar and R. Azhagarasan, 23. New Delhi: Oxford University Press.

Savage, Rowan. 2013. Modern Genocidal Dehumanization: A New Model. *Patterns of Prejudice* 47(2): 139–161.

Straus, Scott. 2001. Organic Purity and the Role of Anthropology in Cambodia and Rwanda. *Patterns of Prejudice* 35(2): 47–62.

Vijila. 2012. The Autobiography of a Bitch. In *The Oxford Anthology of Malayalam Dalit Writing*, trans. Lekshmy Rajeev and eds. M.V. Dasan, V. Prathiba, Pradeepan Pampkirikunnu and C.S. Chandrika, 39–40. New Delhi: Oxford University Press.

Waller, James. 2002. *Becoming Evil: How Ordinary People Commit Genocide and Mass Killing*. New York: Oxford University Press.

CHAPTER 2

Unmade Subjects: Embodiment

Iskander Harappa, the dictator in *Shame*, is tortured in a chamber that Salman Rushdie calls an 'inverse womb', the 'dark mirror of a birthplace'. It is an inverse womb, says Rushdie, because, unlike the womb where life is being made and nurtured, Iskander is 'unmade' (2011: 231). In Alan Cumyn's *Man of Bone*, Burridge thinks of his situation (incarcerated, tortured): 'I'm back in the womb and it feels like shit. Like my body's been cracked and broken and repacked and I just have to get smaller and smaller. Reverse birth' (18). Both texts suggest a reversal or inversion of the growing and birthing process, an 'unmaking'.

'Unmaking' is a term that the noted commentator on torture, Elaine Scarry, used in her *The Body in Pain* (1985) to speak of the unravelling of the body and its universe through torture. This emphasis on unmaking worlds and unmade bodies is at the heart of HR literature because they implicitly signal the collapse of the *subject* of HR.

Human Rights depend on the assumption of a legal subject of those rights. This legal subject is self-determinate (i.e., conscious of the self), meaningful and responsible (Brugger 1996). The legal model of personhood consists of three foundational ideas: the capacity to bear a legal right, a biological body and a responsible subject (Naffine 2009). Anna Grear argues that 'human rights need *redirecting* towards the embodied, vulnerable human being' (2010: 3, emphasis in original). Elizabeth Anker, before pointing to the paradoxes in the liberal construction of the HR subject, notes that 'the dignified individual in possession of rights is

P.K. Nayar, *Human Rights and Literature*,
DOI 10.1057/978-1-137-50432-6_2

imagined to inhabit an always already fully integrated and inviolable body: a body that is whole, autonomous, and self-enclosed' (2012: 3). However, Anker writes, in order to generate the 'dual conceits of human dignity and bodily integrity', liberalism requires the 'threat of bodies being violated, broken, and defiled' thereby entailing that 'human rights discourses and norms are ironically vindicated by inverse images of corporeal unmaking and abuse' (4).

My argument in this chapter continues this line of thought, arguing that HR literature is predominantly concerned with the destruction of the subject. Such a destruction of the subject, the chapter proposes, is mapped out in the theme of the unmaking of bodies and the worlds in which the bodies are embedded. It proposes, following the arguments made by Turner, Judith Butler (2004, 2009), among others, that embodiment and ontology are *social* embodiment and ontology, and that for embodiment to flourish it requires a sustaining, liveable environment. Butler puts it this way: 'there is no life without those conditions that variably sustain life, and those conditions are pervasively social, establishing not the discrete ontology of the person but the interdependency of persons' (2009: 19). Bryan Turner elaborates the contexts in which the possibility of the growing, autonomous and coherent self is located when he identifies the self as constituted through embodiment, enselfment and emplacement. Writes Turner:

> In the process of this embodiment, we also develop a reflexive self that is always expressed *through* embodiment. Our selfhood is reflected in the peculiarities of our own embodiment; our eccentricity is articulated through these practices and our habitus. Two processes—embodiment and 'enselfment'—express the idea that mind and body are never separated. Who we are is a social process that is always constructed in terms of a particular experience of embodiment. Suffering (a loss of dignity) and pain (a loss of comfort, which we need in order to feel secure and confident) are always intertwined, and so vulnerability is both a physical and spiritual condition. Finally, our experience of the everyday world involves a particular place, a location within which experiences of the body and of our dependency on other humans unfold. (2006: 27, emphasis in original)

It is embodiment, enselfment and emplacement that are undermined, and undermine in turn, the subject in specific HR novels. Instead of the subject of HR they present to us unmade bodies, inverted selves and unliveable worlds.

Within HR literature, the theme of unmade bodies, inverted selves and unliveable worlds is most forcefully articulated in a subgenre of the novel, what this chapter designates as the HR torture novel, although texts like Ariel Dorfman's play *Death and the Maiden* also develop a similar theme. The HR torture novel includes Alan Cumyn's *Man of Bone* (1998), J.M. Coetzee's *Waiting for the Barbarians* (1980) and *Disgrace* (1999), Lawrence Thornton's *Imagining Argentina* (1991), Gillian Slovo's *Red Dust* (2000), Achmat Dangor's *Bitter Fruit* (2001), Farnoosh Moshiri's *The Bathhouse* (2001), Vyvyane Loh's *Breaking the Tongue* (2004) and Omar Rivabella's *Requiem for a Woman's Soul* (1986), among others. These novels are characterized by accounts of intimidation, torture, rape and excessive violence directed at 'breaking' individuals incarcerated in prisons and camps. They are novels that show us violated bodies and eroded subjects, dehumanized individuals and collapsed everyday worlds. If the HR novel depicts the subject or person deserving of HR in keeping with philosophical and legal ideas about personhood (Brugger 1996;Naffine 2009), the HR torture novel delivers up a subject who deserves her or his rights to be defended precisely because she/he is no longer an autonomous, coherent or even rational subject after torture. As Turner puts it:

> Human rights abuses disconnect and destroy the conditions that make embodiment, enselfment, and emplacement possible. They typically involve some attack on the body through torture and deprivation, an assault on the dignity of the self through psychological threat, and some disruption to place through exclusion—imprisonment, deportation, seizure of land, or exile. (27)

The HR torture novel, then, presents subjects whose subjectivity has been destroyed and whose story, if we adopt Michael Ignatieff's proposition that a HR campaign can only begin when one *denied* her rights narrates the story of such a denial (2001), implicitly signals the need to protect subjects. Thus, *contra* the *bildungsroman*—which, in his pioneering work *Human Rights, Inc.*, Joseph Slaughter (2007) sees as 'ratifying' (52) human rights by focusing on human development as the 'working-out of the state/citizen bind' (94)—the HR torture novel demonstrates the end of self-determination, the loss of responsibility (even over one's body) and dignity, the awareness of one's person as restricted to a sense of pain, guilt and shame and the untrustworthiness of the physical and social world in which one is located. In the HR torture novel we have a subject whose very subjectivity has been ripped apart, in its body, sense of self, dignity, memories and consciousness. In lieu of the *bildungsroman*'s growing, self-aware, socially competent subject, the torture novel gives us the *inverted* subject.

At the centre of this process—of the making of the inverted subject—is the 'abject embodiment' (Waskul and van der Riet 2002) that renders the subject inverted. Abject embodiment captures both, the broken, corporeally incoherent body and the debased, undignified and grotesque one. Debasement is inextricable from corporeal disintegration, and the sense of the *self*, of its dignity, is at stake when the body is violated.

Painful Bodies

'My torturers were not interested in degrees of pain. They were interested only in demonstrating to me what it meant to live in a body, as a body, a body which can entertain notions of justice only as long as it is whole and well'. This is the Magistrate's account in *Waiting for the Barbarians* of his experiences during incarceration, an account that sums up the abject embodiment of the human (126).

Abject embodiment begins in most cases with the scene of arrest. This is the scene of Susana's arrest in Omar Rivabella's *Requiem for a Woman's Soul*:

> Six men dressed in army fatigues burst into the living room, knocking over everything in their way. Mama and I got to the living room in time to see one of the soldiers strike my father on the head ... Two of the men pushed mama into the bedroom, and the others jumped on me. One of them covered my head with a thick hood while the other two held me ... They wrestled me to my feet and pushed me out of the house. I stumbled over the unconscious body of my father. (Chapter III, entry titled 'January 6')

Mrs Sizela describes her son, Steve's, arrest in *Red Dust*:

> They came in the middle of the night: they always did that as well. They hauled Steve out of bed and handcuffed him. I could see the metal cutting into his flesh and the blood beginning to run as they dragged him out of the house. When he fell down they kicked him and then they hauled him up and threw him to the back of the van. (51)

Lydia is raped in her home, with her husband, Silas, 'chained in a police van, screaming like a madman' outside in *Bitter Fruit* (13–14). And later she is brought to the van and they are both taken away. In *The Bathhouse* Moshiri writes:

> One of the five guards was a young boy, maybe even younger than me ... Their commander, a bearded man, stocky and pot-bellied, ordered the kid to follow me to my room and guard the room when I got dressed. Meanwhile, the other guards ransacked the living room, Mali's room, the kitchen, and the study. They pulled most of the books off the bookshelves and threw them on the floor ... I reached under my skirt to see if I was bleeding, but the boy kicked open the door, jumping into my room ... I realized that he had been watching me getting dressed ... The guard slapped him [her brother, Hamid] on his mouth. (13–15)

In each case, the arrest sequence focuses on the body of the individual arrested but announces its total and immediate subjugation to authority even within the space of her/his own home.

It is an embodiment out of place when the space and the body are both violated as a preliminary to the tortures to follow. Abjection is the effect of rendering the individual's body into an excess, grotesque and ugly—brutalized—in its own legitimate space. That is, abjection and its 'brutish suffering' (Kristeva) begins when the body, which belongs in/to that home is purged violently from the home as a preliminary to its disfigurement and debasement. The home becomes the site of expulsion, violent and brutal so that the individual is rendered a stranger—unrecognizable through the rape, beatings and injuries—within the safe space. Stepping over the father's unconscious body, watching a sibling or parent being assaulted, hearing a partner being raped, watching a son being beaten unconscious—abjection renders all members of the immediate family fungible, all equally expellable from the home as wastes, or wasted, bodies. If the abject is what belongs and yet does not, which must be expelled so as to retain the purity of the body, in the case of the HR torture novel, the violation of the body within its home is what renders it contaminated and therefore the abject. Its connection with the home, the affective ties that bind the body/individual to the home is broken forever when the family sees the body broken, battered and debased (alongside the ravaging of the home-space). The home/house and its emotive and other flows that construct and complete the embodied identity of the subject are rendered into waste. In *The*

Bathhouse Ferial, the protagonist's sister-in-law, whispers to her when they are forced into the police van: 'Don't worry … They'll let you go. Pray for me, I'm pregnant!' (15). The moment is poignant: the conduit for the family's continuity, embodied in the pregnancy, is the most vulnerable. It is no longer just Ferial's body but the family line that is suddenly rendered abject: to be expelled from the home/womb.

Abjection, and the wasting of the body that marks this form of embodiment, begins when the individual first meets the irreconcilable force of the Other. In the HR torture novel the first blow against the subject targets the body and corporeal integrity of the *person*. Jean Améry writes about this first blow:

> The first blow brings home to the prisoner that he is *helpless,* and thus it already contains in the bud everything that is to come. One may have known about torture and death in the cell, without such knowledge having possessed the hue of life; but upon the first blow they are anticipated as real possibilities, yes, as certainties. They are permitted to punch me in the face, the victim feels in numb surprise and concludes in just as numb certainty: they will do with me what they want. (27, emphasis in original)

From this moment onwards the individual's embodiment is the site and cause of its own erosion.

Large segments of the HR torture novel are devoted to the collapse of the embodied subject through *corporeal disintegration.* Since embodiment is the point of departure for the making of the subject (Anker, Turner) of HR then the destruction of this embodiment signifies the erosion or inversion of the subject. This disintegration is accompanied by disfigurement and debasement. If embodiment is central to the HR subject, then the HR torture novel offers up *abject* embodiment. Abject embodiment, Dennis Waskul and Pamela van der Riet argue, following the work of Julia Kristeva, is about damaged bodies:

> Abject embodiment is a state in which coherent bodily boundaries erode and the self has little control over the leaking of blood, urine, feces, vomit, bile, pus, and various other hideous body fluids. Its untidiness violates not only biological but also normative boundaries. What is ordinarily inside now comes out, not only threatening the concretion of the body but also resulting in an ominous seepage of matter of physical, personal, moral, and social significance. (2002: 487)

Thus, along with corporeal disintegration, we see pain resulting in the abject *subject*. Take for instance an account like this:

> Bone. It's all I have left. Rigid, fleshless, jutting bone. Man of bone. Breathing bone. Breathing man of bone. Hood off, shackles off, in the dark with the maggots and the mosquitoes, with my chills and aches, my brain going yammer yammer yammer. And these bones ... Here I am in the reaches of hell, indestructable [sic] man of bone. They can't kill me. *I can't be killed.* No, nothing so simple. I can be starved, beaten, shocked, humiliated, kicked, taunted, degraded, ground into the gravel and taken away by the shovelful. *But I cannot die.* Man of bone for all time, doomed and cursed to suffer with my eyes open.

This is Bill Burridge narrating through considerable pain, his state as a hostage who is regularly tortured during an extended period of incarceration in Alan Cumyn's *Man of Bone* (113–114, emphasis in original). Rivabella's novel portrays women reduced to sexual objects, raped at will, and with astonishing brutality, by the captors. In Vyvyane Loh's *Breaking the Tongue* as Claude Lim's torture proceeds he dehumanizes himself, splitting his self into Claude the Body and his self: 'They have begun the dangerous game of mapping out the Body with knives. Two soldiers, their hands somehow delicate and pale, cut rivers and roads in its skin' (187). And later in *Breaking the Tongue*: 'You make a sound to get their attention and a groan emerges from the Body' (246). And: 'Claude the Body is eating. The rice is giving him strength, even though it's excruciating for him to open his mouth. Every time he attempts it, the cuts on his face reopen and bleed ... He learns it is impossible to chew without moving the muscles of his face' (304). In *Waiting for the Barbarians* the Magistrate is hoisted up in the air by ropes fastened around his wrists:

> I am weak as a baby, my arms come up behind my back, and as my feet leave the ground I feel a terrible tearing in my shoulders as though whole sheets of muscle are giving way. From my throat comes the first mournful dry bellow ... I bellow again and again, there is nothing I can do to stop it, the noise comes out of a body that knows itself damaged perhaps beyond repair and roars its fright. (132–133)

The Magistrate infantilizes himself ('weak as a baby') and then animalizes himself when in pain. I shall return to the animalization theme in HR literature soon.

Unlike the traditional novel that draws us the portrait of an embodied subject, the HR torture novel maps abject embodiment through dismemberment and disfigurement of the subject. Thus Cumyn's description merges bodily disintegration with the psychological-mental one, where the unmaking of the conscious human mind is linked with the unmaking of the corporeal body. Jean Améry famously said about torture that it *reduces* the human to the body:

> Only in torture is the transformation of the person into flesh become complete. Frail in the face of violence, yelling out in pain, awaiting no help, capable of no resistance, the tortured person is only a body, and nothing else beside that. (33)

Yet, this reduction to the body is not simply to that of a flesh-and-blood structure, but to a painful, hurt and damaged body.

In Loh's account, Claude seems to step out of his tortured body, in a move that Waskul and van der Riet anticipate: 'corporeal irruption can alienate the self from the body' (494). Given that Claude no longer has any control over his body, his sense of selfhood is no longer located in this body during such moments. Thus, the process of torture at once *disappears* the coherent, integrated body by rendering it open, visible and a spectacle. Burridge's bone, jutting, fleshless is the opening up of his body to viewing, a viewing over which he has no control. Steve Sizela's mother's memory, in *Red Dust*, of the night of Steve's arrest has to do with such a visibility of the otherwise invisible interiors of her son's body: 'I could see the metal cutting into his flesh and the blood beginning to run' (Slovo 52).

Disfigurement is the opening up of the wounds—*vulnus*—on the body that the torture novel documents in considerable detail. It portrays the reduction of the subject to an object (for the torturer) and a subject defined by pain. Broken bones, damaged faces, eyes closed shut after beatings are commonplace portraits in the HR torture novel. The viewing of corporeal disfigurement is 'performed' by captors, rendering the man or woman an exhibit in their most intimate details.

In the theatre of torture, the 'centre of the scene is occupied by a suffering body, a body reduced to a totally available object, or, rather, a thing objectified by the reality of pain, on which violence is taking its time about doing its work' (Cavarero 31). The passage of time in the HR torture novel marks the erosion of the self.

First, time ceases to make sense for the tortured. In *The Little School* Alicia Partnoy tries very hard to document the passing of time in incarceration and through torture: 'If I'm not mistaken, today is April 16th. February makes me wonder whether I'm wrong. I can't remember if this is a leap year. If so, I have been here ninety-six days' (113). The speaker in *The Bathhouse* wonders after her first session: 'It seemed I had missed a couple of meals. I also wished I knew how much time had passed since they cuffed my wrists behind my back. Was it the same day or the next day?' (68). In *Man of Bone* Burridge's progressive deterioration forms the core of the novel although he can only measure his body's increasing dissolution of time passing, for, as he thinks: 'I'm in the no-time place' (8). Violence takes its time reducing him to 'bone'. In Omar Rivabella's *Requiem for a Woman's Soul*, the progression from beatings to rape and electric shocks and to the final execution takes a long time. In Saadat Hasan Manto's nightmarish tale of the Partition of India, 'Open It', Sakina who has been gang-raped over a period of several weeks, is more a zombie than a human at the end of the experience. After rescue, and during the medical examination, the doctor orders 'open the window'. The semi-conscious girl hears the order and 'moved her hand painfully towards the cord holding up her salwar ... slowly, she pulled her salwar down' (1994: 72). Here Sakina's semi-conscious response to the word 'open' is founded on the experience that she has undergone. The word is a trigger to the rape-victim, who has begun to see *herself* only as a sex-object, and whose body must be made available when the word is enunciated. The point of the tale is not simply that she is in semi-conscious mode, but that her traumatic experience is extended even after the events. In a sense, the event of the rape has altered her for a lifetime, when the very enunciation of the word 'open' is likely to trigger this response. Her time after the event is forever shackled to the event in unconscious repetition. She stays alive within the unending time of the events, so to speak.

When Burridge says 'I cannot die' it effectively means he will be kept alive for further and greater torture, to endure more pain. On another occasion he notes:

> Crying, sobbing most of the time. Nothing to do. Long stretches of when they don't come back—when I don't want them to come back—but there's the fear and terror of waiting. When they strap me in again ... Burning, crackling, searing from inside, like everything ripped open. Different every time, but the same. (52)

'It's all happened before', Burridge thinks, just before they use the electricity on him, and: "I have already lived through it and this is past, this is different time now, I don't have to relive it' (74). Waiting for the sound of her captors, when she hears the 'key slip into the lock', says Susana in *Requiem for a Woman's Soul*, she 'wet her skirt' (chapter V, entry titled 'January 14'). She records:

> I estimated that it was early evening when I started to hear the cell doors opening and prisoners being dragged through the corridor. I held my breath, fearing that my own door would be opened next. (chapter V, entry titled 'January 14')

Alex in *Red Dust* had wished for death, and knew that 'they [his captors] were all-powerful: only they could grant it to him. And that they had refused. They had kept him no longer a man ...' (206).

Second, tortured life is the very opposite of the process of self-fashioning because it marks a slow erosion of the self. Torture in these texts is not just the reduction of the subject to flesh but about the *protracted* extension of pain and the slow erosion of the body's form and attendant dignity, sense of self and identity. Scarry refers to 'the site of entry and the slow motion progress of the widening wound (123) in descriptions of death in battle, but this captures the slow dying of the tortured as well. This slow violence that marks the horrorism of the HR torture novel is achieved through the repetition of torture and the increasing dissolution of the sense of time in the captive. If the *bildungsroman* maps the growth of an individual self over time, the HR torture novel shows how the self collapses with time precisely because the time of torture is immeasurable and unquantifiable. It is the incremental destruction of the body rather than death that marks the HR torture novel, dying rather than death itself.

Thus, subjects are unmade not only due to the torture but due to its repetitiousness, its unpredictability and its timelessness. The individual is beaten again and again. He or she cannot predict when the next session would be. The individual loses all sense of time in the prison/camp. If the body offers the individual agency because it can function in time and space to achieve certain results, torture by its repetition, unpredictability and timelessness erases this agency. I propose that abject embodiment is the effect of the slow, often very slow, deterioration of the body's coherence due to protracted tortures. During the torture session, of course, one is outside time: nothing exists but the immediate pain. But the point I wish to make is that in order to effect the complete decay of any sense of bodily coherence the torture-system inflicts progressive damage on the body. It is rarely sudden: this inverts the subject because it *reverses* the sequence through which the body has come up to this point, built up protein by protein, bone by bone. It is possible that at any moment, with any specific torture-event, the individual could die. So in a sense, the incarcerated are prepared for death constantly, but do not die.

Undignified Bodies, Debased Subjectivity

Central to the abject embodiment in the HR torture novel is the loss of dignity, autonomy and sense of self. Corporeal disintegration is very often accompanied by the loss of sovereignty and autonomy of the body. Pain, commentators tell us, is a subjective experience but which is invested with personal and social meanings (Wuskul and Riet 502–503). Grief and anguish accompanying pain have meaning as well: in abject embodiment the subject realizes that s/he has no longer any power, autonomy or even humanity left. Due to the pain, the victim's mind can no longer determine the choices made by the subject, because the subject is reduced and limited to the immediate body.

Abject embodiment signifying debasement and the loss of dignity occurs through various processes in the HR novel.

The individual emplaced in conditions of debasement is eyewitness to her or his own dehumanization. Kelly Oliver pointing to the paradox of eyewitnessing one's own dehumanization writes:

> The heart of the paradox is that oppression and subordination are experiences that attempt to objectify the subject and mutilate or annihilate subjectivity, that is, your sense of yourself, especially your sense of yourself as an agent. Rendered an object, the victim of oppression and subordination is also rendered speechless. Objects do not talk. Objects do not act. Objects are not subjects or agents of their own lives. (2001: 95)

In Alicia Partnoy's *The Little School*, she documents her intense awareness of her condition:

> I thought that my mind, relieved of its weight [through starvation], would travel in the direction I wanted. But the experiment failed. I was expecting that my psyche, lifted to the ceiling, would be able to observe my body lying

> on a mattress striped with red and filth. It didn't happen quite that way. Perhaps my mind's eyes were blindfolded too. (49)

In contrast to Claude being just the Body in *Breaking the Tongue*, here we see Partnoy's narrator eyewitnessing her state of filth and disrepair, which adds to the sense of debasement. Partnoy constitutes herself as observing agent, as subject in the midst of the very process that objectifies her.

Debasement in the HR torture novel occurs around the processes of two fundamental human actions: *consumption* and *excretion*. Both involve a certain animalization, with the latter focused more sharply on filth and accompanying (animal) revulsion. In both consumption and excretion, food and filth become signs of the victim's animality and attendant loss of humanity. Animality also involves, in addition to such corporeal debasement, the erosion of autonomous choices, the collapse of moral decision-making processes and consequent sense, in the victim, of shame and guilt in the face of mockery by the captors/torturers.

Dalit writing from India is filled with images of hunger, a structural condition of many communities in India. Reduced to starvation by lack of employment, social security and utter poverty, entire families die out or live in the zone of indistinction between life and death. Desperate with hunger, Raghavan Atholi's protagonist in the poem 'Kandathi', sits 'by the garbage in the street', her 'guts burning with hunger'. The Dalit labourers on the fields have their 'waist cloth pulled tight/over a half-filled stomach'. Their 'tears dropping on/the withered faces of/famished babies,/nursed with milk and tears' (2011: 345–346). In Sukirtharani's poem, 'Poem of My Village', she speaks of the 'tormenting starvation' of Dalits and the 'thick sulphurous smell/of the fermented gruel' which is the reward the labourers receive at the end of the working day when their hands are 'abraded' by the plants they cut (2012: 27). Vijila's poem 'The Autobiography of a Bitch' opens with

> We in the street
> Amidst garbage
> Hungry, hungry
> Smelling the chewing gum
> Someone chewed and spat out...
>
> (Vijila 2012: 39)

Dalit stories also highlight hunger as the recurrent motif in the lives of villagers. Shyamal Kumar Pramanik's 'Survival' depicts a family of Dalits who are in a state of near-starvation, seeking to extract rice grains hoarded by rats. The problem is, the rat hole is now occupied by a venomous snake. Despite the pleas of his son and wife, Raj the protagonist is intent on procuring the grain. After a dangerous battle with the snake, Raju manages to capture and evict the snake and reaches into the rat hole for the precious grain. The epic confrontation is for a handful of grain which, Raju claims, will help them survive: 'We'll eat to our full for two days!' (2012: 145). That humans are reduced to scrounging for food grains among the rats and vermin, often at risk to their lives, suggests the continuous exposure to debasement and death that they live with.

During his imprisonment and torture, the Magistrate in Coetzee's *Waiting for the Barbarians* is reduced to an animal state, begging or scrounging for food: 'I can usually wheedle out of the maids the leftovers from the soldiers' supper, a bowl of cold beans or the rich scrapings of the soup-pot or half a loaf of bread' (139–140). Scrounging and eating *like* animals, Susan Derwin notes, was part of the debasement process in concentration camps (75). More importantly, hunger in the victim is a major sign of vulnerability. Maggie Kilgour writes:

> [B]odily needs also indicate that the appearance of autonomy is an illusion, for the body must incorporate elements from outside itself in order to survive. The need for food exposes the vulnerability of individual identity, enacted at a wider social level in the need for exchanges, communion, and commerce with others, through which the individual is absorbed into a larger corporate body. Eating is the most basic of all these needs. (1990: 6)

In the HR torture novel food plays a central role in the debasement of the tortured. 'I live', says the Magistrate in *Waiting for the Barbarians*, 'like a starved beast' (136). And: 'I build my day unreasonably around the hours when I am fed. I guzzle my food like a dog. A bestial life is turning me into a beast' (87). He thinks of food often (97, 105). Burridge describes his state as 'hunger—constant, gritty, greedy' (66). Rivabella's Susana in *Requiem for a Woman's Soul* complains: 'they gave me nothing to eat or drink' (chapter III, entry titled 'January 10?'), 'I haven't had anything to eat for the last two days' (chapter VI, entry titled 'January 17'). When she is finally given an apple to eat, her 'stomach … unaccustomed to such feasts' is 'racked by violent cramps' (chapter XVII, entry titled 'January February 16'). In *Red Dust* after Alex has been tortured to the point of breaking, his reward is Kentucky Fried Chicken. At the Truth and Reconciliation

Commission (TRC) hearing, Dirk Hendricks the policeman who had broken Alex reminds him: 'You were hungry. Remember? I stopped and brought you Kentucky Fried Chicken. You said it was the tastiest food you ever had … Remember?' (192–193). Soon after this Hendricks reminds him: 'I bought you a Coke … We joked about how you were going to pay me back' (194–195). Hendricks evokes Alex's memory of that food, for which Alex had been *then* grateful, to remind Alex, now in the TRC, of his humiliation. Alex of course immediately recalls his humiliations. Slovo writes: 'the man whom Dirk Hendricks had created sat numbly in his seat (193–194). In recalling food, Hendricks forces Alex to recall his humiliations, pain, betrayal—and the man he became when in prison.

If eating and food, rather than processes of survival, become domains in which the human is debased, excretion is equally a site of debasement.

Processes of excretion and waste disposal are all either denied or kept to an intolerably low minimum in the everyday life of the victim. Being covered in one's own shit, vomit and urine, with lice and vermin crawling over the broken body marks the corporeal debasement of the victim. There were no proper receptacles for human waste. Corporeal filthiness, then, is integral to the abject embodiment of the human in the HR novel, and contributes to the animalization of the human because the human is forced to defecate in public, stay unwashed and remain covered in filth.

Alicia Partnoy in *The Little School* documents how the guards watched while the women inmates defecated, being refused toilet paper, and on one occasion, finding her slipper caked in her own waste (30). In *Imagining Argentina*, the brutalized Cecilia, 'when the door opened the following morning … pushed herself back in the corner, not recognizing the sounds she heard as coming from herself' (48–49). Or Silvio 'will imagine his own astonished voice making unfamiliar, animal-like sounds' (141). Debasement into animal-life or through the deployment of animals is a common practice in the HR text. The Magistrate has to perform tricks and realizes that 'there is no way of dying allowed me, it seems, except like a dog in a corner' in *Waiting for the Barbarians* (128). And:

> Nevertheless, I am not taking easily to the humiliations of imprisonment. Sometimes … finding as I pace the room that I am counting *one-two-three-four-five-six-one-two-three* … or brushing my hand mindlessly over my face, I realize how tiny I have allowed them to make my world, how I daily become more like a beast or a simple machine … Then I respond with movements of vertiginous terror in which I rush around the cell jerking my arms about, pulling my beard, stamping my feet. (92–93)

In *Disgrace*, a novel that complicates the lives of humans and animals, Lucy, having decided to hand over herself and her farm to Petrus says about her decision:

> Yes, I agree, it is humiliating. But perhaps that is a good point to start from again. Perhaps that is what I must learn to accept. To start at ground level. With nothing. Not with nothing but. With nothing. No cards, no weapons, no property, no rights, no dignity.
> [David Lurie]: 'Like a dog.'
> [Lucy]: 'Yes, like a dog.'
> (205)

Susana watches horror-struck as dogs are set on the victims' bodies in *Requiem for a Woman's Soul* (XVII). 'I can treat you like a man or I can treat you like an animal', is what Dirk Hendricks used to say, recalls Alex in *Red Dust* (128). Interestingly, the perpetrator, Dirk, is also perceived as an animal. Watching him on the stage during the TRC hearing, Sarah Barcant thinks: 'It was like watching a wild thing ... an animal bound by a past that had brought it to this place' (232). He 'narrowed his eyes' and watched 'through the slits of his vision' with eyes 'bleached to grey' and in a 'voice equally cold' hedges his answers (218–219). Later, Sarah again notices the narrowing of his eyes (325) and imagines how his tortured victim, Alex, might have experienced the policeman: 'now she saw him as Alex must have done, his hard, unfeeling exterior, those eyes, no longer blue but grey. Cold grey. Ice grey. Death grey' (325).

Alicia Partnoy records her thoughts at the imminence of the next round of torture in *The Little School*:

> No, please don't come ... I'm not an animal ... don't make me believe I am an animal ... but that's not my scream ... That's an animal's scream. Leave my body in peace. I'm a little frog for my daughter to play with. (95)

Tabitha, when furious at what she sees as Deng's quiescent attitude towards the white Americans screams at him: 'You're not a person to them! You're an insect! Take control' (Eggers 464). Later, Deng would describe himself as an 'insect' (502). To Elizabeth in *Sandcastle Girls* the Armenian women look like 'dying wild animals' (13). The children in the camp 'huddle, hollow-eyed and sick in their own excrement and filth' (152–153).

The animal is the absolute other to the human in the HR novel: a form of life that can be maimed, killed and annihilated with impunity, for which filth and degraded forms of everyday life are routine. In *Waiting for the Barbarians*, the Magistrate notes that Colonel Joll has a hammer in his hands, and screams at the latter: 'Not with that … You would not use a hammer on a beast, not on a beast!' The so-called barbarians, classified as the 'enemy' before their beating (115), are tied through their mouths and hands to wooden poles and their neighbouring prisoners. They lie 'hands clasped to their faces like monkeys' paws', notes the Magistrate even as he is being beaten (117). Debasement manifests in the theme of an animalization of the human but is closely aligned with the control theme: the animal is wild, unruly and must be controlled—as seen in the passages above, where the animal is beaten, tied and brutalized in an effort to 'domesticate' or tame it. In *Elizabeth Costello* Coetzee makes the explicit link between the victims of the Holocaust and animal genocide:

> They [Holocaust victims] went like sheep to the slaughter … They died like animals … The Nazi butchers killed them … Denunciation of the camps reverberates fully with the language of the stockyard and slaughterhouse that is barely necessary for me to prepare the ground for the comparison I am about to make. The crime of the Third Reich, says the voice of accusation, was to treat people like animals. (64–65)

Here of course the extermination of animals and humans is animalization writ large.

Reduced to animal-like states, the 'inhuman' behaviour, appearance and odours of the victims reinforces their further animalization at the hands of their captors. In *Red Dust* a part of Dirk Hendricks' continued torture of Alex is to call the latter's attention to his physical appearance. Narrated in italics as a metaleptic recall of the events in prison, Slovo has Alex recall Hendricks' remonstrations to Alex:

> Wash yourself.
> You're filthy.
> You want another hiding?
> You stink.
> You disgust me.
> Wash yourself. (127)

In Rivabella's novel the soldiers comment that Susana 'stinks like hell' (Chapter III). She and the other prisoners are not allowed to go to the bathroom and 'by the second day the smell of urine and feces was unbearable' (chapter III, 'entry titled January 10?'). In *Bitter Fruit* Lydia, years after her rape, believes she can smell Du Boise, even when her husband Silas is around: 'I can't rest peacefully with both of you around, your bodies, your smells have become all mixed up' (123). Worse, she 'remembered smelling Du Boise's scent on the baby, a faint stench, the premature decaying of a man' (120). Debasement in Lydia's case is the persistence of the memory of unacceptable smells. In *Man of Bone* Burridge is 'in the dark with the maggots and the mosquitoes'. He has 'running sores' and an 'itchy' beard, attesting to his filthy state (113). On another occasion he is 'stuck in his own vomit for the umpteenth time' (151). 'I have to empty the bucket too. It stinks in here. I want to wash the floor. I want to wash my clothes too,' pleads the Magistrate with his wardens in *Waiting for the Barbarians* (97). 'I lie in the reek of old vomit,' says the Magistrate on another occasion (126). Colonel Joll mocks him with his degraded state: 'Believe me, to people in this town you are not the One Just Man, you are simply a clown, a madman. You are dirty, you stink, they can smell you a mile away' (124). The narrator of *The Bathhouse* describes her state: 'I remember peeing on myself. I remember the foul odor rising from other boxes' (164).

Daily habits and everyday functions serve, in such conditions, to induce the sense of embodied debasement, of humiliation. Humiliation is the meaning the tortured gives her or his pain. Abject embodiment is the interpretation of inflicted pain as the erasure of all control over the world, over decision-making and sovereignty. As Wuskul and van der Riet put it: 'All the grand and complex symbols that define who we are may ultimately rest on the precarious perch of a body that we hope will not obliterate the self through loss of control, grotesque disfigurement, or both' (509). In the HR novel this loss of control and grotesque disfigurement is precisely what unmakes the subject.

Such a debasement through abject embodiment is also achieved by the system when the victim becomes witness to her/his *own* dehumanization. From the consciousness of one's own vulnerability revealed through the primal screams generated in the torture, the victim becomes aware of having soiled herself, of having become an animal. Debasement here is the sense of shame experienced by the tortured. Susana records her dehumanization on scraps of paper using blood and faeces and Father Antonio who receives her account, when opening the package, 'is assaulted by an intense odor as of a mixture of urine and human excrement' (I). Susana literally inscribes her corporeal dehumanization onto paper.

A process that is closely aligned with the loss of corporeal control and dignity—the animalization inflicted in the domains of food consumption and excretion—is the collapse of autonomy choice-making. The HR novel shows how, in the victim of torture, despite the mind's determination to stay in control, the body's needs override conscious choices, moral values and ethical decisions. Thus when Claude is offered a drink, Loh records: 'You don't trust it, would prefer to refuse, but the Body betrays, as usual. It nods eagerly, juts its chin out for the glass that is headed its way' (224). In *Man of Bone* Cumyn gives us Burridge's thoughts:

> I plan it over and over. The next time the water comes I'll refuse it—shake my head, just have a bit, spit that out when they've gone … But then the hours stretch on and, dizzy as I feel, I still want the water … I haven't the will to give it up … Not enough will to refuse the water when it comes … I plan it, but it doesn't matter, when the water comes I open my cracked lips and the relief is nearly too much to bear … I want to refuse but I can't. (66)

Silvio, on his very first day of imprisonment in *Imagining Argentina*, writes Lawrence Thornton, was 'willing to say anything, to disgrace himself, if that was necessary, or implicate innocent people' (141). *Red Dust's* key theme is Steve Sizela's betrayal of Alex, or vice versa, that the Truth and Reconciliation Commission seeks to establish. Betrayal and debasement are intimately connected to the corporeal as well, as we have seen in the case of Burridge and Silvio. In *Red Dust*, Alex recalls his betrayal by Steve as an embodied memory:

> Alex did remember. Not with his mind but with his senses. What his mind had once rejected, his body retained: the tearing of a jaw wrenched open, his flailing skin, the paralysis of fear … That moment of stillness and of clarity replaced by rage when he saw Steve standing by the door and Steve's pointing finger … At that moment he [Alex] had been ready to do to Steve as Steve had done to him: he was ready to betray his friend. (205–206)

Later, when discussing the context of Steve's death the lawyers representing Alex and Steve's parents, Sarah and Ben take different views of Alex's role in the death. Ben says 'Alex must be allowed to come to terms with his own responsibility'. To which Sarah's response is: 'Alex … broke under torture. How can there be any shame in that?' (319–320). In Turkish poet Nazim Hikmet's 'Letters from a Man in Solitary' the inmate confesses:

It doesn't make me blush
That right now
I'm this weak,
This selfish,
This human simply.
(In Forché 499)

Sukirtharani's poem 'Night Beast' captures the debased sense of self of a woman forced to entertain men despite her best intentions:

It was then that the daily
—Unwelcome—visit
Came to pass.
Even as I was watching,
It stripped me away
And brought forth
Another version of myself.
(Sukirtharani 2011: 314)

HR literature demonstrates how both, the ethical dilemma of betrayal and the guilt of debasement, are primarily about abject embodiment: that the subject, no matter however he/she might have determined to be strong, breaks when the body breaks. Torture and prolonged suffering ensures, as Hannah Arendt argued in *Origins of Totalitarianism*, the termination of the moral person because all decisions of the conscience or ethical thinking are equivocal and questionable (Bar On 2002: 101–102). To be forced into the betrayal of one's family or friends or, as in the case of Cecilia in *Imagining Argentina*, being forced to choose her daughter's rapist from among the soldiers, is to be forced through abject embodiment into the abandonment of the moral frames by which human beings live. It ensures that the tortured no longer has the certainty of being able to take decisions of the conscience in interrelations. The sense of betrayal experienced by the tortured also, therefore, turns around the condition of abject embodiment because it is her/his own body that betrays. Elaine Scarry has argued throughout her work on torture that in the process of torture the victims' language, body and mind are turned against them (1985). Even before the self, it is the body that betrays, if betrayal is what it is. Alex regrets that his body could not take any more: 'If only I'd more control'. Then Slovo switches to the third person to reiterate: 'if only he'd more control he could have discharged his hero's duty. He could have chosen death' (206).

Elsewhere Alex remembers 'his voice, craven, pleading for mercy' (133). Cecilia in *Imagining Argentina* also signs documents simply to avert, or stop, what was being done to her:

> Finally she signed something, disgusted by her weakness and unaware that no one can resist forever. Nothing was as important as stopping the men from raping her' If it had only been the pain from the electric shocks she thought she could have resisted, but she could not bear the men's hands on her body. (48)

The narrator's sister-in-law Ferial also eventually gives in and admits that she has reformed in *The Bathhouse*: 'Take me among yourselves and bless me,' she pleads (54). Ferial speaks the language of the torturer—of benediction, of vision and of 'seeing the true light'—in an attempt to end her own torture, just as Alex (supposedly) gives up the names of his comrades during his torture.[1]

The HR novel maps the collapse of the sense of self onto the collapse of the body's boundaries and coherence. Waskul and Riet note about the grotesque bodies of cancer patients: 'like the boundaries of the physical abject body itself, symbolic boundaries may burst and the grotesque stigma extends out, affecting the entire scene of interaction and all participants who interact with "it"'(499). In the HR torture novel the loss of bodily control is accompanied by the cries, whimpers and screams of the tortured subject, which then become the materials for the mockery of the wardens and torturers. Elaine Scarry has proposed that

> he [the tortured] will, while being hurt, be made to speak, to sing, and, of course, to scream—and even those screams, the sounds anterior to language that a human being reverts to when overwhelmed by pain, will in turn be broken off and made the property of the torturers. (49)

The torturers, Scarry writes, use the noises made as a means of another punishment or recording it to be made audible to other members of the tortured's family as a mode of tormenting them. Scarry pays attention to the breakdown of language in the structure of torture. However, the impossibility of confessing or even communicating with the captors in the absence of language is also a form of debasement. For instance, in *Man of Bone*, Burridge does not speak the local language of his captors and his captors do not understand English. Consequently the victim, Burridge, is unable to answer their questions annoying them even further and causing them to amplify his tortures. In *Requiem for a Woman's Soul*, Susana does not ***understand*** the questions the guardians throw at her. This is the case of the protagonist in *The Bathhouse* as well. Abject embodiment here includes the collapse of the primary form of social interaction: the absence of language.[2]

I propose that the mockery of and extended punishment to the grotesque body, that is itself the result of torture and violation, becomes the breaking of symbolic boundaries of human dignity and therefore of the sense of self of the torture victim. Recognizing that each of her or his cries fuels laughter, further pain and contempt ensures that the last shreds of interhuman relations that are foundational to subjectivity are lost, and the subject collapses. Jean Améry notes:

> the expectation of help, the certainty of help, is indeed one of the fundamental experiences of human beings ... In almost all situations in life where there is bodily injury there is also the expectation of help; the former is compensated by the latter. But with the first blow from a policeman's fist, against which there can be no defense and which no helping hand will ward off, a part of our life ends and it can never again be revived. (28–29)

Indeed, in the HR torture novel human relations are built around the vulnerability of one person and the limitless power to injure on the part of the other. The HR torture novel portrays exactly this in its breakdown of the interhuman relations in the prison/carceral and *then* the reversal where, instead of help, the neighbouring human becomes either the instrument of greater injury or the point from which mockery originates so as to demolish the trust individuals place in the world.

In *Waiting for the Barbarians* the Magistrate describes how he 'does tricks for them [the torturers]'.

> They stretch a rope at knee-height and I jump back and forth over it ... I baulk. The point of the cane finds its way between my buttocks and prods. 'Jump,' Mandel murmurs. I run, make a little skip, blunder into the rope, and stand there. I smell of shit. I am not permitted to wash. The flies follow me everywhere, circling around the appetizing sore on my cheek ... I skip ... It gives me agonies of shame the first time I had to come out of my den and stand naked before these idlers or jerk my body around for their amusement. Now I am past shame ... each time I discover with surprise that after a little rest, after the application of a little pain, I can be made to move, to jump or

> skip or crawl or run a little further …There is no consoling grandeur in any of this. When I wake up groaning in the night it is because I am reliving in dreams the pettiest degradations. (127–128)

In Moshiri's *The Bathhouse* the protagonist is shackled. And then:

> She pulled my right arm over my right shoulder, then twisted and stretched my left arm from my waist to my shoulder blades.
> "You're breaking my shoulders," I pleaded.
> "Don't! It hurts!"
> "Really?" She said and they both laughed. (64–65)[3]

In *Requiem for a Woman's Soul* when Ana and the handcuffed women scream abuses at the guards, one of them 'turned up the radio to full volume'. Then 'who the hell is going to hear you?' asks the guard (chapter V, entry titled 'January 14'). 'Even my screams were his instrument,' cries Lydia in *Bitter Fruit*, recalling her rape (17).

When the vulnerability and helplessness embodied in the grotesque body, covered in injuries, body fluids and waste, becomes the spectacle for the entertainment of the torturers, the tortured reaches the absolute bottom of debasement.

The frames of reference—bodily functions, bodily borders with the world, agency to perform an action—for locating a sense of the self are destroyed and the subject begins to see her/himself only in terms of pain and disintegration. Since the body is the first site of subjectivity, it also becomes the site of subjectivity's repression and erasure, the site of power and discourses that make or unmake this subjectivity. The destruction of the body conveys the limits of the individual and the structures of power—apartheid, totalitarian states, civil war—within which individual subjects live. That is, even when the HR torture novel presents the broken body it is in fact locating this body within systems of power relations, the larger habitus of the subject beyond the body.

The HR novel also ensures that we see the individual and the entire key question of rights as contextualized, set within particular worlds and institutions. That is, the HR novel moves outward from the individual subject of HR to a social ontology, to the self-in-the-world. Commentators such as Judith Butler (2004, 2009) and Bryan Turner (2006) have argued that we need to see individual subjects as subjects-in-the-world, constituted by their interrelations and dependency. The HR novel in its representation of social ontology demonstrates how the subject of HR is destroyed because he or she no longer lives in a world that sustains life.[4]

Embodiment and Proximate Grief

Debasement might follow betrayal and sense of shame induced through the process of torture. Debasement as a constitutive component of torture marks the erosion of corporeal integrity and sense of self. HR literature also offers another mode of the destruction of the sense of corporeal self, and this through the assimilation of another's grief. Enselfment demands a certain amount of empathetic identification and proximate grief is one route into enselfment in HR texts. 'Proximate grief' is my term for the intercorporeal self that is destroyed through the forced viewing of another's torture, especially that of a family member's, a friend's or in some cases, even a stranger's.

This connects with the emplacement theme too in a very particular way: other bodies occupy the same world of the subject, and their destruction induces panic, anxiety and loss of faith in the sustainable world. Starting with the family and immediate social settings, the HR torture novel maps the disintegration of the world in which the individual is embedded. This involves setting up a triangulation of the victim, her or his family/friends/comrades and the torturer to show how the world of relations, especially secure relations (made of family/friends/comrades) is undermined.

Grieving for the missing or dead loved ones and a persistent anxiety over the fate of their loved ones characterize the interrelations of the collapsing subject world in the HR novel. Proximate grief is the condition introduced into the process of torture, imprisonment and disappearance wherein an individual, or group of individuals, is forced into a situation of grieving for a loss or injury or even the imminent *threat* of injury and loss. 'Proximate' designates the bond holding the individuals together but also gestures at the proximity of threat of this injury to somebody the prisoner loves or knows.

In the first weeks of his detention Burridge assures himself:

> They didn't really get Maryse and Patrick. I know they didn't … I know it for a fact. For a fact. (16).
>
> They didn't get Patrick or Maryse. They're safe. They're back in Canada now. (18)

He worries they might 'go after Patrick' (55).

The Sizela family in *Red Dust* mourns their son, whom they cannot also fully mourn because they have never seen his body or given him a proper burial: 'All James [Sizela] wanted was his son. His son to bury before he himself grew too old to do so' (47). Alex continues to grieve for his act of betrayal, under torture, of Steve: 'There's more than one way to bear responsibility. I might not have struck the blow, but what I said was as deadly as if I had. Through my words I sentenced Steve to death' (330). Both the Sizela family and Alex are trapped in the unsustainable world of betrayal and ignorance. The family cannot obtain their son's body, and Alex is never sure whether he was directly responsible for Steve's death.

In the very first pages of *Breaking the Tongue* we see Claude beaten and tortured. But the word 'afraid' is first used to describe his condition when he hears a woman's (perhaps Ling-li's) screams from the next cell: 'then the scream again. A woman's scream, you realize, and this time, you are afraid' (22). The 'again' suggests the torture in the next cell has been going on for some time, but Claude begins to be afraid only when he recognizes it to be a woman's scream. As the narrative will reveal later, the woman is Ling-li and Claude is forced to hear her being tortured. Susana records in *Requiem for a Woman's Soul*: 'I started to think about my parents and Nestor. I fell into profound despair. I cried uncontrollably' (XXI). She is threatened by one of her captors: 'Think of your parents. Isn't it worth the life of your parents, the little cooperation I'm asking from you? Or the life of your boyfriend, Nestor'. And she screams 'No … no' (XXXV). It is no longer the torture of her corporeal self alone that troubles her. Susana records:

> I no longer care what they do to me. When they mentioned my parents and Nestor, they smashed to bits the shield I had used to protect my soul. They have forced me to confront the idea of horror endured by those I love. I know that today they will come for me again. But I don't care. My parents are suffering. Nestor is suffering. (XXXVI)

In the S.H. Vatsayan (Ajneya) story of the Partition of India, 'Post-Box', the protagonist opens his narration with expressions of anxiety over his family's safety:

> There was no member of my own family with me in the refugee camp, but I did meet people who knew the whereabouts of each of them … A man can

> endure the greatest of calamities if he can say, "No one dear to me suffered". (Vatsayan 1994: 105)

Part of the genocidal savagery of the Partition was a particular mode of humiliation inflicted by both Hindus and Muslims on each other. In Intizar Husain's 'City of Sorrow', the three ghosts of men massacred during the riots exchange notes. One man speaks of how, at the point of a sword, he forced a young man to strip his own sister in public. But the subsequent events are even more tragic. The ghost reports:

> I lived to see the young man repeat what I had done. He caught a woman in a burqa who was running away in fear. The old man with her pleaded: 'O young man, have pity on us ...' The young man's eyes burned red with rage as he shouted—Is she related to you? The old man replied—Son, she is my wife. Grinding his teeth together, the young man ordered—Old man, strip her naked ... Intoxicated with rage, the young grabbed the old man by his neck and screamed.(1994: 85–86)

Carlos sees in his visions in *Imagining Argentina*, Hirsch, one of the recently arrested, about to be tested: 'they plan to take one of his children and put a knife to its throat and then test Hirsch's belief in the names' (160). Cecilia herself in the same novel is forced to witness her daughter's suffering:

> The room would be close enough to the one where they kept Cecilia so that she could see the guards taking Teresa in and out, could see the terrified expression on her daughter's face. The guards would want her to hear the screams when they applied the belts, or hoses, or wires.(129)

Later Cecilia's torture consists of being forced to choose which captor could rape her daughter in the adjacent cell: 'choosing is part of your punishment,' she is told (155).

Proximate grief for the loved ones, then, is the constituent of subjectivity in the HR torture novel, especially because this grief is linked to the recognition that the loved ones are fungible with the individual being tortured in the present. When Burridge worries that his captors may find his son Patrick or his wife Maryse he experiences panic attacks and absolute grief. That is, even in the midst of his pain and in his deteriorating mind, Burridge acknowledges that all members of his family are fungible. Cecilia in *Imagining Argentina* fears for her daughter, who later joins her in the adjacent cell. In *The Bathhouse* the narrator of the story worries about her brother and sister-in-law even as she herself awaits further beatings.

The tortured is thus drawn into the theatre of cruelty as the third party (after the torturer and the tortured), the witness, to the torture of her or his family member. When Susana first hears and then sees Nestor, her lover, drawing his breath in agony after torture, she becomes the witness to his dehumanization (*Requiem for a Woman's Soul*). When Silas is forced to listen to the screams from his wife (*Bitter Fruit*), he is an unwilling witness as well. In *The Bathhouse* the narrator reports: 'Mrs. Moradi … told me in a whisper that all day yesterday they had hanged her son upside down from the ceiling and had forced her to watch' (98). Rubén in *Imagining Argentina* is in a cell from which he can hear his wife Marta screaming in an adjacent cell (62). Social and familial relations, as Görling points out, rely on forms of expression (67), which violence disrupts or even replaces. That is, we can see torture as the interruption in the forms of expressions that constitute the very fabric of social and familial relations. Violence is inscribed into the relation of mother and daughter (*Imagining Argentina*), wife and husband (*Bitter Fruit, Imagining Argentina*), mother and son (*The Bathhouse*), among others, thus reordering the relation itself where each is forced into the (additional) role of eyewitness—to their loved one's dehumanization, either in the present or threatened in the future.

Grief and the fear for the well-being of the loved ones function as the frames within which the tortured perceives those *other* lives. That is, the HR novel offers a different frame of apprehending lives of loved and proximate ones: that of precarity (Butler 2009). The Sizelas (*Red Dust*), Susana (*Requiem for a Woman's Soul*), Burridge (*Man of Bone*), Cecilia (*Imagining Argentina*), Lurie (in *Disgrace*), the 17-year-old inmate in *The Bathhouse* and Silas (*Bitter Fruit*) find their proximity to particular individuals as the source of anxiety, shame and guilt. The tortured is drawn into an unwilling, fearsome and grieving spectatorship of their friends, comrades and loved ones being subject to pain and debasement. The torture novel therefore transforms the security of specific relationships into the instrument of their collapse by converting proximity into *shared* precarity and imminent fungibility. I shall return to this theme of *witnessing* vulnerability and victim fungibility in a later chapter.

I propose, then, that the HR novel triangulates relations around proximate grief thus: victim-torturer-family. By pointing to grief and fear as the dominant codes informing this schema, the HR novel offers up an entirely new view of sustaining relationships and subjectivity-through-empathy of the subject. The torturer mediates between victim and the family, and the destruction of one, either victim or family, ensures grief for the other.

But in other HR texts this (ap)proximation and assimilation of another's grief as a way of enselfment becomes both slippery and indeterminate. The protagonist who is released from prison at the end of *The Bathhouse* may have been raped because she is informed while still in prison:

> Leila had heard that they raped the virgins before execution. Because if they killed them as virgins, they'd send them straight to heaven. They wanted to send them straight to hell. (93–94)

But the narrative leaves it open-ended whether she is raped or genitally mutilated. Susana's family in *Requiem for a Woman's Soul* never know the extent of her torture—including rape—because her document is not shared with anybody except Father Antonio who goes mad after the experience of reading it. Claude in *Breaking the Tongue* hearing screams from the adjacent torture chamber might be hearing Ling-li being raped, but the text does not specify the nature of her torture except to indicate that it is extensive.

In these cases of gendered violence, unlike in the 'regular' torture text, the violation of the woman is not always accessible as proximate grief. HR literature dealing with rape suggests that allowing the woman's grief to become proximate to another's might be not be easy. In such texts it is the personal, completely inaccessible grief that might be agential subjectivity, as seen in the case of Lydia (*Bitter Fruit*) and Lucy (*Disgrace*).

The unshareability of pain and grief, even with family members, is also a theme in several HR novels. For instance, in *Bitter Fruit* when Silas informs Lydia that he saw and met her white rapist Du Boise earlier in the day, she is shocked. (Silas had been shackled inside the police van outside their house while Du Boise raped Lydia.) Silas tries to explain that he understood her pain. She retorts: 'You don't know about the pain. It's a memory to you, a wound to your ego, a theory … You can't even begin to imagine the pain' (14). The family drifts apart over the inability to share the pain from long ago. It is almost as though the event of rape, from over a decade ago, has determined the path the family has to take. Eventually, of course, we discover, along with Mike (Lydia and Silas' son), that Mike is the son from that rape. Rape thus renders the family apart, but what Lydia grieves over is Silas' wilful forgetting of the event although he had been an earwitness. She grieves over the loss of intercorporeal subjectivity when she says: 'You don't remember the pain. It's a memory to you, a wound to the ego, a theory … You don't remember my face, my tears' (14). Lydia is accusing Silas of having been there and yet *not* there when he recalls the horror.

A similar emphasis on the unshareability of the pain that destroys the intercorporeal identity of the (masculine) subject may be found in *Disgrace*. Lurie pleads with his daughter to leave the Eastern Cape, or to tell the police, but she insists: '*You don't know what happened*' (134, emphasis in original). Later Bev Shaw reiterates Lucy's comment to Lurie: 'But you weren't there, David. She told me. You weren't' (140).

Lurie does not *see* his daughter being raped (*Disgrace*), and Carlos is not even in the prison where his wife Cecilia is raped (*Imagining Argentina*). Claude does not *see* Ling-li's rape. Silas hears Lydia's screams but cannot *see* the rape. We are not told if Nestor witnesses Susana's rape in *Requiem for a Woman's Soul*. Susana leaves behind her testimony but Ling-li dies. Lydia and Lucy both refuse to speak about their violation. In both *Disgrace* and *Bitter Fruit*, proximate grief is the representational silence around the woman's violated body, conveying the impossibility of ever knowing what the violation meant to the woman. It hovers just out of reach of words and representation between Lucy and Lurie, Lydia and Silas, Cecilia and Carlos.[5]

Dangor, Loh and Coetzee offer us a wholly different view of the proximate grief generated in witnesses and loved ones by the other's abject bodies: an awareness of the *secret* carried by the woman's body. For the men, even when they are fellow-victims, the very nature of abjection, and its possible representation are different. The woman, on the other hand, does not fit into the available representational schemes for her abjection. In the case of male victims, writes Louise Bethlehem, the 'abject body has been made to foreshorten the distance between trauma and its representation so that the trauma of the victim might appear to speak itself without mediation' (2003: 175). But the case of Lucy presents a different abjection:

> Externally unmarked in the immediate present, but marked otherwise, marked over time, by pregnancy, Lucy's body does not carry the stigmata of visible injury, for her body has, I claim, a different message to convey. Her pregnant body becomes the site where the immediate passage between

> violation and its visible effects, its most accessible 'meaning' in the masculinist economy is delayed, deferred, suspended. (176)

In Lucy's case there is a pregnancy as the sign of her rape, and in Lydia's case Mikey is the child of the rape. Carlos and Cecilia have lost their daughter, Teresa, to torture in *Imagining Argentina*. For both Lurie and Silas, then, the child of rape represents both, the scar the woman will perpetually carry (as opposed to the man's scars from the tortures) and the embodiment of the scar in the form of a child. Both novels mark proximate grief as continuity, or an embodied continuum, stretching from the scarred past to the scarred future.

The unshareability of grief in these texts is *gendered* so that it is the scarred woman who occupies centre stage, and the men can stand by, proximate, but ultimately unable to know what the past violation has *really* meant, what Bethlehem in the above passage describes as 'delayed, deferred, suspended'.[6]

Whether the woman's (ruined) subjectivity lies in the memory of her rape or in the agential silence adopted by Lucy and Lydia is an arguable point. But what emerges in these two cases is that the raped woman refuses to allow her pain to become accessible and assimilated into another's subjectivity, as Lydia makes clear:

> I cannot speak to Silas, he makes my pain his tragedy. In any case, I know that he doesn't want to speak about my being raped, he wants to suffer silently, wants me to be his accomplice in this act of denial. I also cannot speak to my mother and father. They too will want to take on my pain, make it theirs ... They will also demand of me a forgetful silence. (127)

Lucy says to Lurie in *Disgrace*: 'you don't understand what happened to me that day ... Because you can't' (157). She is emphatic that nobody else might appropriate, for whatever purposes, her story: 'The reason is that, as far as I am concerned, what happened to me is a purely private matter. In another time, in another place it might be held to be a public matter. But in this place, at this time, it is not. It is my business, mine alone' (112).

Adding a layer of complexity to the question of proximate grief and shared vulnerability, this theme of agential act of silence from the injured woman is depicted as eroding the empathetic subjectivity that the male seeks for himself. Thus Silas is outraged at Lydia's silence in *Bitter*

Fruit and Lurie in *Disgrace* is baffled with fury at Lucy's stubborn non-communication. Lurie's thoughts are as follows:

> *You weren't there. You don't know what happened.* He is baffled. Where, according to Bev Shaw, according to Lucy, was he not? In the room where the intruders were committing their outrages? Do they think he does not know what rape is? Do they think he has not suffered with his daughter? What more could he have witnessed than he is capable of imagining. Or do they think that, where rape is concerned, no man can be where the woman is? Whatever the answer, he is outraged, outraged at being treated like an outsider. (140–141)

Gareth Cornwell writes about Lurie's situation vis-à-vis both Melanie (the student he seduces and then rapes) and Lucy: 'this failure of mutuality, of empathy, of imaginative identification, this refusal to acknowledge the self's necessary passage through the other, seems to lie at the heart of the novel's thematic burden' (2002: 315). Both novels, *Bitter Fruit* and *Disgrace*, I suggest, interrogate the possibility of the intersubjective condition, especially when the situation involves rape. Even the semblance of subjective agency left to the woman after the rape, the novels suggest, not unproblematically, might be better guarded through silence. Ana Miller writes about Lydia's silence in *Bitter Fruit*:

> Lydia feels unable to speak because she thinks her trauma will be appropriated and silenced by those around her. She refuses to allow her deeply personal, intense pain to be managed, contained, or silenced by being absorbed into terms of dealing with trauma that she does not trust. Lydia's written private testimony indicates her rejection of what she envisages would be Silas's and her parents' way of dealing with her rape; she refuses to become an "accomplice" in either "act of denial." (2008: 153)

***

In these texts embodiment is the site of the crisis of subjectivity. Tortured and debased bodies destroy the home of the subject of HR. Attempting proximate grief goes some way towards empathetic understanding and the minimal building of a sense of self, but even this process, as Coetzee and others demonstrate, is riddled with potential risks.

Notes

1. Incidentally, Hendricks in *Red Dust* files for clemency under the TRC, and claims he suffers from Post-traumatic Stress Disorder which resulted in an attempt to strangle his own wife. These actions, the psychologist's report claims, were 'the direct result of the strain of his position [as a policeman]' (129). Alex thinks: 'he left me nothing…Not even my anger' (128). Here the torturer turns victim in the TRC proceedings.
2. A comparable parallel from the contemporary would be the Abu Ghraib torture cultures where, on several occasion, the inmates did not speak English and the wardens did not speak Pashtu or even Arabic. See Gronvoll for two instances of this language issue (2010: 70–71).
3. Torturers laughing at the screaming tortured is documented by numerous survivors in their testimonies, for instance, in *Nunca Más (Never Again): Report of Conadep* (National Commission on the Disappearance of Persons), Argentina (1984), available at http://www.desaparecidos.org/nuncamas/web/english/library/nevagain/nevagain_000.htm.
4. In the process of depicting the fiendish dehumanizing tortures, occasionally authors like J.M. Coetzee also seek to understand the person of the torturer. Perhaps the most sustained examination of the torturer-subject may be found in *Waiting for the Barbarians.* In a short passage the Magistrate ponders over the persona of the torturer:

   > I wonder how he felt the very first time: did he, invited as an apprentice to twist the pincers or turn the screw or whatever it is they do shudder even a little to know that at that instant he was trespassing into the forbidden? I find myself wondering too whether he has a private ritual of purification, carried out behind closed doors, to enable him to return and break bread with other men. Does he wash his hands very carefully, perhaps, or change all his clothes; or has the Bureau created new men who can pass without disquiet between the unclean and the clean? (13)

5. For the Magistrate in *Waiting for the Barbarians*, the suspension of (masculine) knowing and the attendant silence, even when he is saddened by the scars on the blinded, crippled woman victim of the Empire's tortures, is unbearable. This is what he records about his own attitude towards the girl: 'It has been growing more and more clear to me that until the marks on this girl's body are deciphered and understood, I cannot let go of her' (33). Michael Valdez Moses has proposed that the Magistrate's 'solicitous attention to the Other cannot be separated from the sinister apparatus of torture that the Empire employs' (121).

6. I am not here addressing the racialized nature of the gendered violation in each of these texts: the Korean comfort women in *War Trash*, Lucy in *Disgrace*, Ling-Li in *Breaking the Tongue*, Lydia in *Bitter Fruit* and the 'barbarian' in *Waiting for the Barbarians.* Considerable attention has been paid to the race-rape theme in Coetzee's Disgrace (Cornwell 2002; Graham 2003; Kossew 2003; Kissack and Titlestad 2005; Mardorossian 2011).

Bibliography

Anker, Elizabeth S. 2012. *Fictions of Dignity: Embodying Human Rights in World Literature.* Ithaca and London: Cornell University Press.

Atholi, Raghavan. 2011. Kandathi. In *No Alphabet in Sight: New Dalit Writing from South India. Dossier 1: Tamil and Malayalam*, trans. T.M. Yesudasan and eds. K. Satyanarayana and Susie Tharu, 345–347. New Delhi: Penguin.

Bar On, Bati-Ami. 2002. *The Subject of Violence: Arendtean Exercises in Understanding.* Lanham: Rowman and Littlefield.

Bethlehem, Louise. 2003. Aneconomy in an Economy of Melancholy: Embodiment and Gendered Identity in J.M. Coetzee's *Disgrace. African Identities* 1(2): 167–185.

Brugger, Winfried. 1996. The Image of the Person in the Human Rights Concept. *Human Rights Quarterly* 18(3): 594–611.

Butler, Judith. 2004. *Precarious Life: The Powers of Mourning and Violence.* London: Verso.

———. 2009. *Frames of War: When is Life Grievable?* London: Verso.

Coetzee, J.M. 1999. *Disgrace.* London: Secker and Warburg.

Coetzee, J.M. [1980] 2004. *Waiting for the Barbarians.* London: Vintage.

Cornwell, Gareth. 2002. Realism, Rape, and J. M. Coetzee's *Disgrace. Critique* 43(4): 307–322.

Cumyn, Alan. [1998] 2002. *Man of Bone.* Toronto: Emblem-McClelland and Stewart.

Dangor, Achmat. 2001. *Bitter Fruit.* New York: Black Cat-Grove/Atlantic. (eBook).

Graham, Lucy Valerie. 2003. Reading the Unspeakable: Rape in J.M. Coetzee's *Disgrace. Journal of Southern African Studies* 29: 433–444.

Grear, Anna. 2010. *Redirecting Human Rights: Facing the Challenge of Corporate Legal Humanity.* London: Palgrave Macmillan.

Gronvoll, Marita. 2010. *Media Representations of Gender and Torture Post-9/11.* London and New York: Routledge.

Husain, Intizar. 1994. City of Sorrow. In *Stories About the Partition of India*, trans. Vishwamitter Adil and Alok Bhalla and ed. Alok Bhalla, vol. II, 85–99. New Delhi: HarperCollins.

Ignatieff, Michael. 2001. *Human Rights as Politics and Idolatry*. In *Human Rights as Politics and Idolatry*, eds. Michael Ignatieff and Amy Gutmann, 3–98. Princeton: Princeton University Press.

Kilgour, Maggie. 1990. *From Communion to Cannibalism: An Anatomy of Metaphors of Incorporation*. Princeton: Princeton University Press.

Kissack, Mike, and Michael Titlestad. 2005. The Dynamics of Discontent: Containing Desire and Aggression in Coetzee's *Disgrace*. *African Identities* 3(1): 51–67.

Kossew, Sue. 2003. The Politics of Shame and Redemption in J. M. Coetzee's *Disgrace*. *Research in African Literatures* 34(2): 155–162.

Loh, Vyvyane. 2004. *Breaking the Tongue*. New York: WW Norton.

Manto, Saadat Hasan. 1994. Open It. In *Stories About the Partition of India*, trans. Alok Bhalla and ed. Alok Bhalla, vol. II, 69–72. New Delhi: HarperCollins.

Mardorossian, Carine M. 2011. Rape and the Violence of Representation in J. M. Coetzee's *Disgrace*. *Research in African Literatures* 42(4): 72–83.

Miller, Ana. 2008. The Past in the Present: Personal and Collective Trauma in Achmat Dangor's *Bitter Fruit*. *Studies in the Novel* 40(1–2): 146–160.

Moshiri, Farnoosh. 2001. *The Bathhouse*. Seattle: Black Heron.

Naffine, Ngaire. 2009. *Law's Meaning of Life: Philosophy, Religion, Darwin and the Legal Person*. Portland, OR: Hart.

Oliver, Kelly. 2001. *Witnessing: Beyond Recognition*. Minneapolis: Minnesota University Press.

Raj, A. Vincent. 2012. Clutching the End of My Saree. In *The Oxford Anthology of Tamil Dalit Poetry*, trans. Ravi Shankar and eds. Ravikumar and R. Azhagarasan, 23. New Delhi: Oxford University Press.

Rivabella, Omar. 1986. *Requiem for a Woman's Soul*. Trans. Paul Riviera and Omar Rivabella. New York: Random House. (eBook).

Rushdie, Salman. 2011. *Shame*. London: Random House.

Scarry, Elaine. 1985. *The Body in Pain: The Making and Unmaking of the World*. New York: Oxford University Press.

Slaughter, Joseph R. 2007. *Human Rights, Inc.: The World Novel, Narrative Form and International Law*. New York: Fordham University Press.

Slovo, Gillian. 2000. *Red Dust*. Hachette Digital. (eBook).

Sukirtharani. 2011. Night Beast. In *No Alphabet in Sight: New Dalit Writing from South India. Dossier 1: Tamil and Malayalam*, trans. N. Kalyan Raman and eds. K. Satyanarayana and Susie Tharu, 314–315. New Delhi: Penguin.

———. 2012. Poem of My Village. In *The Oxford India Anthology of Tamil Dalit* Writing, trans. Lakshmi Holmström and eds. Ravi Kumar and R. Azhagarasan, 27. New Delhi: Oxford University Press.

Thornton, Lawrence. [1987] 1991. *Imagining Argentina*. New York: Bantam.

Turner, Bryan S. 2006. *Vulnerability and Human Rights*. University Park: University of Pennsylvania Press.

Vatsayan, KH [Ajneya]. 1994. Post-box. In *Stories About the Partition of India*, trans. Alok Bhalla and ed. Alok Bhalla, vol. III, 105–109. New Delhi: HarperCollins.

Vijila. 2012. The Autobiography of a Bitch. In *The Oxford Anthology of Malayalam Dalit Writing*, trans. Lekshmy Rajeev and eds. M.V. Dasan, V. Prathiba, Pradeepan Pampkirikunnu and C.S. Chandrika, 39–40. New Delhi: Oxford University Press.

Waskul, Dennis D., and Pamela van der Riet. 2002. The Abject Embodiment of Cancer Patients: Dignity, Selfhood, and the Grotesque Body. *Symbolic Interaction* 25(4): 487–513.

CHAPTER 3

Witnessing

In Dave Eggers' *What Is the What* Valentino Deng tells us the story of Monynhial, one of the boys walking across Sudan, along with Deng, to escape the civil war. The group had watched five boys die—'three immediately and two others, whose legs had been shredded by the bombs, were alive long enough to watch the blood leave their bodies and darken the earth' (159)—in the course of their walk. Monynhial, after a few days, tells Deng '"I can't be hunted like this"' (159). Deng tries to convince him that he, Monynhial, is safer with the group. But Monynhial decides not to go on. Deng then reports how Monynhial stayed back in a village, digging a hole in the ground and staying inside.

> On the third day he decided to die in the hole, because it was warm there and there were no sounds inside. And he did die that day because he was ready. None of the boys who walked with me saw Monynhial perish in his hole but we all know this story to be true. It is very easy for a boy to die in Sudan. (160)

In *The Bathhouse* Farnoosh Moshiri recounts the days of imprisonment: 'women kept entering the cell and leaving. I was the permanent one … A woman's appearance and disappearance became faster than ever; at least, it seemed faster to me' (144).

Common to both these texts is the narration of events that are not eyewitnessed by the narrator, but to which the narrator testifies. In both

P.K. Nayar, *Human Rights and Literature*,
DOI 10.1057/978-1-137-50432-6_3

cases the narrator is an individual whose corporeal integrity has been violated through torture and deprivation and therefore whose subjectivity is eroded. It is such a subject-in-ruins, so to speak, who testifies to the complete erasure of an-other body, an-other subjectivity and an-other individual.

The protagonists of HR literature, such as the ones in the passages cited above, are often individuals whose subjectivity has been eroded. HR literature positions these individuals not as examples of an evacuated subjectivity but as those who find a measure of subjectivity returning through the specific process of speaking out. Such a speaking out has two dimensions: a narration of their dehumanization in the form of an experiential discourse and self-witnessing (the condition of witnessing one's own dehumanization), and a narration of the dehumanization of an-other, who might not even be in the sightline, in the form of bearing witness. Witnessing is the key process in the rebuilding of subjectivity after the confinement, torture and dehumanization. A quick example at this point in time offers us a way into examining the structure of witnessing.

Alex Mpondo, a scarred survivor of a traumatic period in prison in Apartheid South Africa, in *Red Dust*, agonized by the TRC's proceedings, says to his lawyer Sarah Barcant: 'You know I never wanted to come to this hearing' And then adds: 'If I hadn't been pressurised by James's need and also by *my own need* to lay Steve to rest, I wouldn't have come' (227, emphasis added). Mpondo is gesturing at the sense of response-ability, of bearing witness to Steve's death (in the same prison as Mpondo) so as to retrieve a measure of his own humanity. The 'my own need' in his statement to Sarah serves as a marker of this response-ability as subject re-formation: he is not testifying for the dead Steve—who is the true witness, to the inside of the prison, to apartheid itself—alone, but for *himself* as well. *Red Dust's* narrative, devoted to the examination of testimonial stories illustrates the centrality of witnessing to the re-formation of destroyed subjectivity in the manner Kelly Oliver (2001) theorizes.

'Subjectivity', writes Oliver, 'is the result of the process of witnessing' (7). Oliver proposes that conditions of extreme oppression work to destroy subjectivity by *othering* the individual. Oliver writes:

> Being othered, oppressed, subordinated, or tortured affects a person at the level of her subjectivity, her sense of herself as a subject and agent. Oppression and subordination render individuals or groups of people as other by objectifying them. Objectification undermines subjectivity: to put

> it simply, objects are not subjects. Through the process of bearing witness to oppression and subordination, those othered can begin to repair damaged subjectivity by taking up a position as speaking subjects. (7)

But, as scholarship has established, an extreme situation of oppression such as the Holocaust is usually an 'event without a witness', as Dori Laub famously described it (1992: 75–181). True witnessing can only be from the inside, but there are no true witnesses to such events as described in *Imagining Argentina*, *Red Dust*, *A Gesture Life* and numerous other HR texts. The only witnessing, therefore, is provided by those who were not fully 'inside', those who were not completely annihilated by the process of oppression. Expanding on Felman's work, Oliver writes:

> Felman concludes that it is impossible to testify from inside. From the inside the possibility of address and of an addressable other was eliminated. Yet in order to reestablish subjectivity and in order to demand justice, it is necessary to bear witness to the inarticulate experience of the inside ... We are obligated to witness beyond recognition, to testify and to listen to testimony—to encounter each other-because subjectivity and humanity are the result of witnessing. That is to say, subjectivity and humanity are the result of response-ability. (90)

Later Oliver adds:

> More important, it is through witnessing and reestablishing the inner witness who is damaged by objectification and subordination that we can move beyond repetition of trauma to elaboration and interpretation. The witness, ultimately the repair of the inner witness, allows someone to be both inside and outside her own oppression and victimization at the same time. (92)

Further, this entails bearing witness to an-other's oppression. Oliver argues, this time building on the phenomenology of Merleau-Ponty, that

> I can almost experience something of the other's embodiment ... I can experience the movements of their body in the same way that I experience the movements of my own. More than this, I can feel their effervescence and fatigue. This opening of the boundary between self and other resonates with the theory of biosocial energy. (199–200)

The biosocial energy that Oliver identifies is the circulation of *affective* energies, and plays a key role in the structures of sociality in the HR texts.

Oliver is thus inventorying the modes and effects of witnessing through which subjectivity of the oppressed is rebuilt, and offers us a way of tackling the HR texts in which survivor accounts constitute the bulk of the narrative. In this chapter I build on Oliver's work to argue that HR literature envisions the rebuilding of subjectivities after these have been severely eroded through dehumanization and emplacement in horrific conditions (examined in the preceding chapters). I argue that witnessing is central to this process of rebuilding and, in HR texts, takes various routes and forms. Witnessing generates and channelizes the circulation of affective energies. It is instrumental, through the form of testimonial storytelling, both official and sanctioned (as in TRCs in *Red Dust*, *The Persistence of Memory*, *Anil's Ghost*) or unofficial and vernacular (as in *Imagining Argentina*), in the production of knowledge. It appropriates certain objects, including victim bodies, as melancholy objects that then acquire narrative elaborations in the lives of individuals and communities. It enables the transformation of the abject subject into a political subject.

Witnessing and Heteropathic Empathy

'Vision', writes Oliver, 'is the result of the circulation of various forms of energy, including social energy … Social energy includes affective energy, which can move between people' (8). Examining 'proximate grief' in the preceding chapter I proposed that the HR novel transforms the security of specific relationships into the instrument of their collapse by converting proximity into *shared* precarity and imminent fungibility but not incorporation or assimilation. Proximate grief, I now propose, is not necessarily grief at an individual's loved ones or friends being subject to dehumanization and genocidal rage. I expand the idea of proximate grief in order to propose that witnessing involves a circulation of affective energy between and across individuals trapped in situations of utter hopelessness as well, thus building a sociality among victims. A sociality built on bearing witness to suffering begins with the sense of an affected self. Watching the torture or death of an-other entails a form of *empathic* relation with the other, a relation often born, in HR texts, from having gone through a nearly equal condition of being tortured. This empathic relationality does not demand pre-existing familial or social connections: individuals are brought together in their mutually assured suffering. The affected self is the one *moved* by compassion and/or hopelessness—the two affective states most frequently documented in HR literature—at the sights one sees and apprehends even if one does not actually *see* in the prison. Such a self also develops a sense of response-ability. HR literary texts therefore foreground response-ability as an effect of the empathic relations amongst victims.

Bearing witness in HR literature offers us the circulation of affective energies—empathic relations, as I shall argue—as modes of comprehending and apprehending an-other life and through this come to a recognition of one's own subjectivity. By apprehension I mean 'norms of intelligibility about life' (2009: 7). In the face of the suffering of others, writes Butler, our response to this suffering depends on a 'certain field of perceptible reality ... one in which the notion of the recognizable human is formed and maintained over and against what cannot be named or regarded as the human' (64). I propose that compassion, and the response-ability arising from this compassion, constitute the organization of the field of perceptible reality in which an individual seeks to recognize an-other human precisely in the erosion of this other's humanity. That is, compassion as response-ability is the response of one suffering and impotent individual to another, where the one who bears witness responds to the suffering other as one whose humanity is being destroyed. When in *A Gesture Life* Hata finds the dismembered and brutalized body of K, his sentiments are recorded in terms of frames of ***recognition*** of a human(ity) that is annihilated: 'And I could not know what I was doing, or remember any part' (304–305). This is not a description of his actions—he is gathering her remains—but a statement of witnessing about what is no longer human. This statement is preceded by an account of her 'tiny, elfin form', her 'figured arms and feet', the 'digitation of her hands'—all of which (once) render(ed) her human. Susana in ***Requiem for a Woman's Soul*** records her impotence: 'She [Alicia] frantically searched for my eyes, imploring me to help her. I turned away from her. There is nothing I can do. Nothing I can do' (XXXIX). In turning away Susana recognizes Alicia's loss of humanity even as she records her own impotence as a human to help a fellow human.

The one who bears witness retains the notion of a human precisely because she/he witnesses somebody who/that can no longer be named or regarded as the human. It is in the intercorporeal and affective recognition of the remains of the human in the presence of 'what cannot be named or regarded as the human' that makes for the affective energies binding individuals together.

Kelly Oliver proposes that perception is not the effect of vision alone. Commenting on Merleau-Ponty, Oliver writes:

> vision is proximal in that it is possible because our flesh touches the flesh of the world. It is possible because the world also has flesh. Vision touches the world and people in it not in order to fix it or them in the gaze. Rather, vision is movement, more like a caress than a grip, more like a motion picture than a photograph … There are no gaps between us and the world, since we touch it with our eyes, working as they do in coordination with all of sensation … If vision is part of a sensory system that includes what we take to be more proximal senses like touch, taste, or smell, vision becomes a sort of touching, a palpitation with the eyes. Vision itself becomes a proximal sense. If the eyes are flesh—porous membranes—and not solid mirrors or windows or Lacanian bowls, then vision like the other senses necessitates a type of interpolation of elements that cannot be imagined as an impassable abyss or alienating gap. (202–203)

Thus, Oliver is proposing a model of seeing as proximal rather than distancing, and one that is possible because of the coordination of multiple senses all assaulted by pain and deprivation, and a resultant affective response that might be termed heteropathic empathy.[1]

Isolated and developed as a critical concept by Dominic LaCapra, heteropathic empathy resists identification with the other, and is defined as an 'affective relation, rapport or bond with the other recognised and respected as such' (2001: 212–213). Such heteropathic empathy therefore retains difference but acknowledges similarities of the Other to oneself.

In the case of HR literature the senses most alerted and active are the tactile ones, primarily because of the state of assaulted bodies. The eyewitness bears witness to the erosion of corporeal integrity of an-other by experiencing an assault on her or his own body as well. The resultant affective social energies bind the two sufferers/victims together, watching each other in and *through* pain. The one who bears witness perceives *through* her own pain, framing the collapse of an-other human through the sense of loss of one's own humanity.

HR texts record this circulation of affective energy of compassion and angered impotence that then defines individuals as well as sociality. The texts achieve this by capturing a wide emotional range among the eyewitnesses. In *Requiem for a Woman's Soul* Susana records other victims screaming while witnessing the torture of fellow inmates (XIII). She prays for a woman who is tied to stakes in the grounds and dies slowly (XV).

When Susana sees Silvia—whom the state was trying to find—finally captured and tortured in her, Susana's, presence, she records: 'all the resentment I had felt for her gave way to compassion' (XVII).When Nestor her boyfriend is tortured in her presence, she screams at the torturer: 'Son of a bitch, you son of a bitch ...' (XL). In *The Farming of Bones*, survivors record how they witnessed the brutalization of their family members:

> Only a few paces from me ... they had them tied in ropes and Don Jose, who has known me my whole life, went at them with his machete, first my son, then my father, then my sister. (209)

A sociality built upon heteropathic empathy also binds the boys in the camps in *What Is the What*. The boys are asked to cane each other, and some of the boys were 'enthusiastic', reports Deng. But eventually, each of them having experienced caning elsewhere find a way of coping with the recent disciplinary move and so 'a system was devised whereby the caner struck the ground, not the victim's backside, and caner and canee still made the expected sounds of effort and pain' (329). The stigmatized and tortured identity of each body, subject to torture, starvation and pain becomes the foundation for a heteropathic empathy with other such boys and results in the group deciding on this strategy where, crucially, articulations of affect—the 'sounds' of pain—are produced by the parties. That is, the sounds working in consonance with each other are empathic sounds, each following in or accompanying the other, matching the other so that the caner and canee are within the same continuum, acknowledging the other's difference while admitting to the fungibility of each.

Such documentation of the emotional range within the setting captures multiple witnessing and multiple stories that subtly undermine the possibility of any narrative authority. Instead of narrative authority the HR text foregrounds affective energies circulating and eddying around witnesses. That is, texts like *Requiem for a Woman's Soul* that have narrators recounting multiple perceptions of the events, in the form of multiple emotional responses to the events, provide us a sociality built around the circulation of affective energies. Every victim perceives the annihilation of one other human (except in the case of a text like *Man of Bone* where the narrative deals with solitary confinement). 'Seeing' here is a proximal sense as Oliver notes because the victims began to share the suffering of each other, sensing the other's pain by *having gone through the same pain oneself*. The victim does not take the place of the (suffering) other—indeed one cannot take the place of the other—but recognizes and *feels* (for) the pain of this other. This heteropathic empathy generates compassion in the witness, and in the tortured victim, is a step towards retrieving a sense of being an agent, a subject. Compassion as a theme is the literary articulation of empathy in HR texts.

Lauren Berlant in the Introduction to a volume of essays on compassion writes:

> When the response to sufferings scene [sic] is compassion—as opposed to, say, pleasure, fascination, hopelessness, or resentment—compassion measures ones value (or one's government's value) in terms of the demonstrated capacity not to turn one's head away but to embrace a sense of obligation to remember what one has seen and, in response to that haunting, to become involved in a story of rescue or amelioration. (2004: 7)

But compassion itself, Susan Sontag has proposed, arises out of a sense of impotence at the sight of suffering (*Regarding the Pain of Others*). Compassion and empathy as this sense of obligation, even when born out of impotence, is the assertion, however minimal, of subjectivity where nothing beyond or other than the compassionate sense—as in actual help or support—is possible in the torture chamber or within the oppressive state.

The inability (or prohibition) to express empathy marks the oppressive emplacements of many even within the in-groups, though. In Horst Bienek's 'Exodus' the speaker, perhaps a ghost of a man murdered by the regime/state, asks:

> Who among you, the living can say
> That he saw us?
> Who among you, the dead, can say
> He recognized his brother?
>
> (In Forché 468)

Bienek's speaker is pondering over the nature of the in-group, with its mutually shared experiences, but unable to recognize, empathize and mourn their loved ones and fellow-victims. The 'can say' is indicative of doubt over one's ability, but can also be interpreted as the freedom to 'say', to speak and declare recognition. The speaker might be gesturing at the *contexts* of enunciation.

Witnessing that generates empathy as represented in HR texts is constitutive of the re-formation of the subject because it offers a response to the other victims and engenders a sociality. Throughout *Requiem for a Woman's Soul* and *The Bathhouse*, for instance, Susana and the unnamed narrator are responding to fellow-victims. Within the isolated space of the prison, the inmates are forced into empathic relations, often spilling over into care, with each other. The subjects of HR novels situated within what Suzanne Keen has called 'bounded strategic empathy'. Bounded strategic empathy, notes Keen, 'occurs within an in-group, stemming from experiences of mutuality, and leading to feeling with familiar others' (2007: 142). The 'boundedness' is agential in that individuals respond to fellow-victims and thereby forge a community. Sharing shame, pain and humiliation but not standing *in place of* the other, bounded strategic empathy is at once the source of a minimal subjectivity and communitarian connections in a non-place such as secret prisons and torture chambers. Witnessing the other's pain and responding to it with such an empathic relation offers the tortured a minor agential role, even if this is a token role and preliminary to her or his own complete annihilation (as in the case of Susana in *Requiem for a Woman's Soul*).

Witnessing and Knowledge Production

The HR text offers us the injured human subject, one whose subjectivity has been severely eroded, and who seeks partial restoration of her or his subjectivity. A measure of agency to this injured subject is made available in the HR text through the testimonial *authority* with which s/he tells the story of deprivation, suffering and torture. Furthering the quest for restoration of subjectivity is also about the torture-victim or war-victim producing *knowledge* about the state, apartheid, secret police, tortures and such 'crimes against humanity'.

Testimony itself, as Liran Razinsky reminds us, is a *trope* and not just a fact of reality (2010: 182). HR texts work to establish a certain 'testimonial authority' (James Young's term, cited in Razinsky 182). This process of establishing testimonial authority involves the evocation of memory and the frequent referencing of historical details (183). The process of establishing testimonial authority begins well before the personal, purportedly fictional, story unfolds, in the form of metatextual and intratextual details.

In Moshiri's *The Bathhouse*, for instance, the text is prefaced with a key dedication: 'To the memory of the prisoners of conscience who were executed in the prisons of the Islamic Republic of Iran and to M. Raha, whose memoir inspired this work of fiction' (unpaginated). Dave Eggers' *What is the What* has a map of Sudan prefixed to the text. Tony Eprile's *The Persistence of Memory* gives us two full spread maps of South Africa, one nearly labelled 'Tourist Map of South Africa'. The novel also footnotes army slang, explains acronyms of military outfits, Afrikaans words, local place names, animal life, and so on, throughout (121, 136, 238, and elsewhere) so that it approximates to a different register of narration, and in its Afterword gives a list of additional reading (290). Thornton's *Imagining Argentina* has direct references to the military regime, the name of the country, 'Argentines', the Mothers of the Plaza de Mayo and concludes with the trial of the generals at the end of the 'Dirty War'. Alicia Partnoy's detailed Introduction to *The Little School* gives a synoptic history of the Dirty War and the 'disappeared'. At the end of her narrative she also offers 'Cases of the Disappeared at the Little School', brief accounts of individuals and their time in prison (123–131), a map of the Little School (132) and biographies of the various guards (133–136). Forewords and Afterwords by Ariel Dorfman to each of his plays (*Widows, Death and the Maiden* and *Reader*) situate the fictional worlds in their historical and geographical particulars. One of the endorsements for *Requiem for a Woman's Soul* cautions us: 'this is not a novel about the past horrors of Argentina. It's an urgent and unforgettable reminder that brutish assaults on the human body and spirit are going on even as we turn these pages.' A short paragraph inserted after the dedication in *The Cellist of Sarajevo* informs us that 'the Sarajevo in this is not a novel is only one small part of the real city and its people, as imagined by the author' (unpaginated). The Eileen Julien Foreword to Diop's novel informs us that '*Murambi* was written to bear witness to the Rwandan genocide' (unpaginated). References to 'Empire' and 'conquest' throughout *Waiting for the Barbarians* ensure that we see Coetzee's novel as an allegory for imperialism. David Park's *The Truth Commissioner*, Achmat Dangor's *Bitter Fruit* and Gillian Slovo's *Red Dust* firmly situate their stories within the context of the Truth and Reconciliation Commissions of Ireland and South Africa.

Historical accuracy rendered through both metatextual and intratextual materials ensures testimonial authority to the fictional representation of Human Rights violations. I propose that this metatextual information becomes a key mode of framing the personal stories being narrated within the text. Rather than serving as a façade, maps and historical detailing constitutive of traditional historical discourse become the scaffolding on which the personal trauma and witnessing is hung. Further, historical details and social knowledge make their way into the personal storytelling that constitutes the main text of the novel as well, and is a characteristic of much testimonial and trauma writing, as Robert Eaglestone notes (2008: 79).

One can discern specific consequences of the imposition of testimonial authority.

First, HR literature in its emphasis on testimony and witnessing is founded on an opposition between concealment and revelation, secreting and disclosing. The telling of one's experiences in these texts—whether in the form of Carlos' 'visions' of the tortures in Argentinian prisons (*Imagining Argentina*), smuggled memoirs (*Requiem for a Woman's Soul*), the testifying to TRCs (*Red Dust*, *Bitter Fruit*)—might then be taken to be the revealing of secrets that the state or political system did not wish to reveal. Indeed, the absence of evidence in the form of documents points to the careful erasure of material witnesses, and itself serves as the sign of the effective modes of extermination. German poet Sarah Kirsch's 'Legend of Lilja' describes the problem of evidence from inside the concentration camps. Only legends about Lilja circulate, because the 'testimonies of surviving camp inmates' are 'so contradictory' (in Forché 474). There is no picture of her, and of the seven letters she wrote, six reach 'the one they don't know' and the seventh is 'traded for bread' (474). Although 'all spoke a long time' about her, nobody quite agrees about anything. The poem concludes:

> In the letter was said to be written we
> Will not get out of here we have
> Seen too much (476)

Whether all this was actually written in the seventh letter itself is a matter of speculation, or even wishful thinking. Whether the letter was written by a real woman inmate is also a matter of speculation. In the midst of such speculations, 'she' has become a legend. In short, nothing survives except the *legend* of a letter from a woman who is also, perhaps, a *myth*. The only discordant note in the entire rhetoric of legend and disappeared evidence is what sustains the poem, and HR: that the *stories* of the letters Lilja wrote from camp have survived.[2]

Second, what Susana in *Requiem for a Woman's Soul*, the unnamed narrator of *The Bathhouse*, Carlos in *Imagining Argentina*, the Magistrate in

Waiting for the Barbarians, Paul Sweetbread in *The Persistence of Memory* perform when they document, orally or in scripted texts, the events they experienced and witnessed is a trauma that is theoretically beyond representation and yet must be represented (Caruth). Writing about the storytelling on which the TRCs relied Rosalind Morris states: 'the telling of stories came to function as a mechanism for addressing a trauma that had, under apartheid, consisted at least partly in the exclusion from a sphere of representability' (2011: 395).

Third, as instances of knowledge production these HR texts play a significant role in that they render visible historically obscured and unrepresentable events. In Rosalind Morris' phrasing, 'the fictive works by making the "unbelievable" actualities of apartheid "believable" to the reader who would otherwise disavow them as too improbable' 'illuminate the historical truth' of apartheid, totalitarianism, war, imprisonment and torture (397–398). Eaglestone offers an interpretation of these 'novelized testimon[ies]' (82) as referring to events that are not necessarily 'incomprehensible': indeed Eaglestone detects an 'implicit comprehensibility' (82) to the events narrated. Yet, it must be said that the novelized testimony of HR texts is *one* perspective on colonialism (*Waiting for the Barbarians*), apartheid (*Bitter Fruit*, *The Persistence of Memory*, *Playing in the Light*), genocide and ethnicide (*Murambi*, *The Farming of Bones*, *A God in Every Stone*, *Sandcastle Girls*), war (*The Cellist of Sarajevo*, *War Trash*, *A Gesture Life*, *Breaking the Tongue*) , totalitarianism (*Of Love and Shadows*, *Death and the Maiden*, *Imagining Argentina*) and other extreme socio-historical situations around the world. As Liran Razinsky reminds us,

> The project of testimony is not identical with the historical accuracy of the novel. Historical accuracy is one way to establish testimonial authority for presenting a specific perspective about the Holocaust. (183)

As forms of knowledge production, then, novelized testimonies offer us a specific perspective on comprehensible but otherwise unbelievable events and actions.

This limited and subjective knowledge-making and meaning-making nevertheless is valuable in a certain understanding of the historical. To return to Morris once more, novelized testimonies 'speculate on dimensions of the historical real that remain inaccessible to empiricism and that exceed what might have been addressed if it had not been fully resolved either in a formal legal context or in the pseudo-juridical theater of the TRC' (398). Novelized testimonies, then, *represent* a certain *secret* experience that is *embedded* in the historical real but is not directly empirically verifiable.

I think of knowledge-making and meaning-making in such novelized testimonies as indicative of the reclamation of the subject of HR who has otherwise been muted, disappeared and made invisible in the historical real of apartheid or war. The HR subject in these texts therefore speaks, mostly in the first person or in recorded testimonies (Susana's in *Requiem for a Woman's Soul*, Mpondo's and Sweetbread's testimony before the TRC in *Red Dust* and *The Persistence of Memory*, respectively), in the absence of a place from which any utterance was possible at all: prison, camps, torture chambers. Thus, Deng's first-person account in *What Is the What* is an attempt to claim a position to speak from, where speaking as *witness* to what happened—including being *eyewitness* to the deaths of other boys, assaults, refugee camps—on their long march through Sudan *implies* a subjectivity.

Melancholy Objects and Witnessing

In Slovo's *Red Dust*, Alex Mpondo has a moment where he recalls the now-dead Steve, his former comrade, standing on a platform with his fist raised. Then he wonders: 'was this real memory or was it merely created by the fact that Mpondo had seen that photo hanging in his mother's house?' (170). The photo triggers (false?) memory and mourning, infused with guilt, in Mpondo. From an entirely different perspective about specific objects, Faustin Gasana, one of the Interahamwe killers in Diop's *Murambi*, stares at a portrait of Major-General Juvénal Habyarimana. His narrative records his thoughts: 'the very man that our enemies have just murdered' ('Faustin Gasana'). In Thornton's *Imagining Argentina* and Allende's *Of Love and Shadows*, families of the disappeared turn up in public spaces carrying photographs of their missing children, spouses and siblings. In Ondaatje's *Anil's Ghost* Sarath, just before he is taken away by the Sri Lankan government and killed, records his observations on a tape and buries it inside the dead body that Anil and he were trying to identify and then use as evidence to expose the government's terror.

Photographs and mementoes such as the above in HR texts serve the function of supplementing the witness' subjectivity: these objects are at once essential to the completion of their subjectivity and social ontology as well as an excess. They are melancholy objects, defined by Margaret Gibson as 'objects of the dead—those spectral, melancholy objects mediating, and signifying, an absence' (2004: 285). Such an object functions as a 'memorialized object of mourning' (289). In photographs, on tape and in other such objects, 'the absent, yet representationally, present body' continues to haunt (Gibson 295). Melancholy objects in the HR texts are supplements to witnessing subjectivity because these ensure that the disappeared and the dead are socially and politically alive even if biologically dead. They constitute not only the material metaphoric-metonymic traces of the dead/disappeared but are integral to the self-fashioning of the witness *as* subject. It should be noted that we are not looking at museumized objects—such as the heap of bones in *Murambi* or *Of Love and Shadows*—but rather at *ordinary* objects whose narrative elaborations in the lives of survivors take on a melancholic form as part of their self-fashioning, but also serve other purposes, as we shall see.

In Gasana's case (*Murambi*), the portrait of the dead President becomes not simply a melancholy object, but an object integral to his self-fashioning as a saviour of Hutu pride and purity. The narrative elaboration of the President in Gasana's throwaway comment suggests an entire social discourse built around loss (of a leader) but also around betrayal and treason by ethnic groups. A character in Michel Serumundo's narrative in *Murambi* reads the plane crash that killed the Rwandan President as a 'sign from God' (*Murambi*, 'Michel Serumundo'). Michel Serumundo himself recognizes that the dead President is socially alive, appropriate into a discourse of revenge, purity and ethnic cleansing: 'this time the murderers had the perfect excuse: the death of the president. I didn't dare hope that they would be satisfied with just a little blood' (*Murambi*, 'Michel Serumundo'). Serumundo is pointing to the appropriation of the dead man—embodied in the traces of his portrait that Gasana focuses on at the very beginning of the novel—into the social discourses of the murderous Hutus.

For the young Raami in Vaddey Ratner's *In The Shadow of the Banyan* her father's notebook, in which he used to write poetry, serves as a melancholy object. The father has been taken away, although the family does not know with certainty if he is dead or alive—there are no witnesses ('we didn't even know where Papa had been taken … Where was his grave? Did he have a grave?' wonders the child, 309). The family, shunted out of the palace they lived in, has been relocated to a rural setting. In the notebook that Raami's mother has managed to hide, the father has left a letter. The letter contains the description of a land to the east where 'the sun blazes as red as here' and a land to the west which is a 'land of golden temples'. The letter urges them to 'head west, follow the stars until sunrise' (304). The instructions constitute, the mother says, a 'map' (304). With the appearance of the letter all hope Raami retained of returning to her original home fades, resulting in mourning, when the mother says: 'I thought of going home ... but there is no one there. Only ghosts await us' (304). With the instructions on the map, Raami understands, the mother 'was fighting for my survival while preparing me for my death' (305). On their journey to safety the girl opens her father's notebook again and reads his benediction for her, his hope that she will survive and his funerary prayer for his own soul (311–312). The notebook is at once a melancholy object that induces and evokes mourning in Raami and her mother and a set of instructions—indeed an injunction—to survive. The girl has to survive to tell the story, to bear witness. This function of the melancholy object as a mute witness to the tragedy of genocide and as an injunction to the survivor to bear witness comes across in the very last paragraph of the novel:

> We left this land, Mama clutching a paper boat and a book of poetry, and I the mountains and rivers, the spirits and voices, the narratives of a country that would in turns shade and shadow me on my journey. Its prophecy has become my story. (314–315)

While the 'prophecy' might be a gesture at the 'narratives' of the country, Ratner's Raami might be speaking of her father's notebook in which he urged her to survive. The melancholy object here mediates between the world of her childhood and the world she escapes to. It enables mourning for the father and offers the hope of life (in a very literal sense, by offering a coded map to a different land). Margaret Gibson has proposed that the melancholy object 'transitions in grieving' (289). The notebook Raami and her mother carry transitions from an object that is 'an indirect corporeal contact' with the dead father/husband (289) into a signifier of his last injunction as a father, and of hope. The notebook, as the last paragraph of the novel indicates, will forever serve as a *reminder* to mourn, but also to live.

Towards the end of *The Cellist of Sarajevo* (based on Vedran Smailović's cello playing during the siege), the unnamed cellist finishes playing: he has played every day at 4 PM for 22 days in honour/memory of the 22 people killed when waiting in the bread line.

> After a while he stood up, and he walked over to the pile of flowers that had been steadily growing since the day the mortar fell. He looked at it for a while, and then dropped his bow into the pile … He turned, picked up his stool and went through the door to his apartment without looking back at the street. (256)

The instrument has already been transformed into a melancholy object with the cellist playing his elegiac and beautiful music for the dead. But with this final act the melancholy object acquires a double significance: as an object that helped mourn the dead and as a memorial to the *act* of mourning itself. It transitions and mediates between the dead and the living and embodies the act of secondary witnessing performed by the cellist.

In the course of the hearing at the TRC Alex Mpondo in *Red Dust* continues to assume that Steve Sizela had indeed betrayed his comrades during torture. Until one day when Mpondo goes out to a distant farm and digs out the 'dead letter box'—the location for leaving communications for comrades. In the tin box Mpondo finds a scrap of paper with the name of a comrade, 'of a man who was never picked up by the police' (172). This discovery sets off a train of rationalizing in Mpondo accompanied by a memory of the broken Steve outside his (Mpondo's) cell in prison, pointing (173). This pointing Mpondo assumes was Steve's gesture of betrayal—'Alex was convinced that his old friend Steve had broken, had betrayed not only him but also all their hiding places' (173)—and remains 'Alex's most dominant memory of Steve' (173). Then Mpondo thinks:

> If Steve had broken, he would have needed information to show he was telling them all he knew … he would have told them about the dead letter box. But if they knew about that they would have picked up the comrade who was implicated here. Doubt surged through Alex's mind … was it instead possible that Steve had never talked? … A single thought: Steve, what did I do to you? (173)

The disintegrating tin box with the crucial paper, from this point onward in the novel, serves as a melancholy object for Mpondo. The box serves as a mute witness to Steve Sizela's innocence, and to Mpondo's own guilt at assuming Steve's guilt. It is a witness that appears late on the scene by which time Mpondo has already borne witness to Steve's supposed betrayal. Alex Mpondo had lived with this question in his head: 'Steve's death: his fault?' (133). The tin box indicates to Mpondo that Steve had indeed not broken under torture but perhaps Steve's death was Mpondo's fault, that Mpondo had assumed Steve's betrayal. As a melancholy object the box initiates and drives Mpondo's mourning. It also serves as a reminder of his having borne false witness, to his eagerness (under torture) to yield information: 'he hadn't just told Dirk Hendricks where to find the guns, but had offered up the information as a gift, accompanied by other words ... *please ... I'll tell you anything*' (192, emphasis in original). As a melancholy object the tin mediates memories, grief and guilt. It alters the way Mpondo remembers Steve, for instance, and his own self-fashioning as a man who gave up information because he believed he knew Steve had already betrayed them all. Thus, it is a melancholy object for the role it plays in Mpondo's witness: in his hand it is a mute witness to his (false) belief of several years, of being betrayed by Steve *before* he, Mpondo himself, betrayed the organization. Having fashioned himself as a late-betrayer, the tin reveals to him that his self-fashioning was predicated on a lie and this induces the melancholy. Mpondo's political subjectivity—as anti-Apartheid fighter, as torture-survivor—begins to collapse under the weight of this new witness.

In another case a melancholy object is introduced in order to establish the innocence of a mass-murderer, such as Major Lyddie in Eprile's *The Persistence of Memory*. Paul Sweetbread, the protagonist, has photographed Lyddie's murderous carnage and the stacks of dead bodies (249–251). However, at the TRC a photograph is produced that captures Lyddie 'rescuing three African kids while under fire' (255), with only Sweetbread who understands that, while the photographic evidence is 'quite impressive', 'the photographers couldn't have gotten there until hours later' (256). In other words, the evidence furnished is actually false and testifies not to Lyddie's massacres but to an entirely different incident. The photographic 'evidence' produced in favour of Lyddie's heroism serves as a 'melancholic object' where, these supposedly capture life (or lives saved) and not death, rescue and not ruin—yet it functions, as Sweetbread recognizes, as a cover-up for Lyddie's murderous actions. That is, the *staged* photograph of his supposed rescue mission serves for Sweetbread and him alone as a reminder of what Lyddie *actually* did. The photographic objects are melancholic because, for Sweetbread, the 'evidence' of Lyddie's life-saving act reminds him of the deaths the man perpetrated. The doctored photograph intervenes between his actions (massacre) and his enactments of certain other actions (rescue). The staging of a heroic Lyddie in the evidence drives Sweetbread's memories (unvoiced) to the actual progression of events but also, simultaneously renders his voiced memories as 'the product of a fevered imagination' (256). In other words the photographs of the heroic Lyddie offer the official and juridical counternarrative to both Sweetbread's memories and Sweetbread's own photographs, disproving both. Sweetbread's memories and photographs both *reveal* Lyddie as a murderer, and thus portray the dead as killed. The melancholic object signifies those dead who are not recognizable as victims because the only story that counts, by virtue of the 'evidence' produced, is that of Lyddie's heroism.

The melancholic object that is the doctored photograph—in the sense, the photograph is from a different place and time—produced at the TRC represents Lyddie in a wholly different manner and this automatically converts the massacred and the dishonoured bodies of the enemy—a violation of Geneva Conventions—into what the novel calls 'a particularly bad case of suicide' (248). Thus melancholic objects, as the HR novel depicts them render the victims of the white soldiers biologically and socially dead. That is, the deployment of the 'heroic' photograph in the TRC testimony successfully depoliticizes the bodies of the victims of the army action. Those killed had already been objectified once—as 'things' to be deprived of their lives with no compunction—and with this move, they are objectified yet again.

If in one case the melancholy object enables the self-fashioning of the perpetrator, it generates nostalgia and mourning for the dead/disappeared in others (individuals, families and entire communities) and finally, functions to annihilate all subject-positions through a double objectification in some others. The corpse mutilated and buried in an unmarked grave on Lyddie's orders, is merely a figure, denied the rites, rights and modes of disposal of dead bodies—thus rendering them into ungrievable lives. It is the doctored photograph that, inserted between action and enactment of action, 'produces' this state of death for the black soldiers in *The Persistence of Memory*. Melancholy objects are integral to the process of witnessing because they acquire narrative elaboration in the lives and deaths of subjects. In some cases, such as the cello in *The Cellist of Sarajevo*, it might come to represent both mourning and the memory of mourning for an entire community.

There is another form of the melancholy object that makes its presence felt in several HR texts: the broken body of the victim. Being disabled, ruined, scarred and mutilated, the victim represents the material witness, the corporeal testament of a regime's processes. I see these as instantiating the traumatic process but also as metonyms of a cultural ruin. By bringing the body back into the discourses of witnessing, the HR text ensures that we understand that sites of memory, sites of meaning and sites of testimony are essentially *corporealized.*

In *Requiem for a Woman's Soul* Father Antonio visits Susana's house after he has finished reading her account of imprisonment and torture. There he finds the girl's father sitting in an unventilated room staring at a jar. Inside the jar, Antonio discovers,

> were two hands, severed at the wrist. One of them bore a ring on the middle finger. Together they floated in the bloody liquid, in a macabre ballet. There was Susana's engagement ring. (XLI)

The ring is of course a melancholy object but it is the severed hands that constitute the 'true witness' for whatever happened to Susana. There is not even an entire body to mourn or bury, just a horrific metonym. Alicia Partnoy in *The Little School* writes about how when she was cold she was given a denim jacket to use. She recognizes the jacket as belonging to another inmate, Vasca, who had been killed. The jacket is first referred to as 'magic' although she acknowledges that 'Vasca, who used to wear it, was taken away' (109). Immediately after this account, Partnoy speaks thus of the jacket: 'the burden on my heart shattered into a thousand pieces that are still running through my blood today, a thousand drops of bitterness … I cried again' (109–110). Partnoy invests the jacket with some magic but also melancholic memories of the previous wearer. She 'recalled the times when [she] peeked under the blindfold to see Vasca' (110). At one point she believes that the 'jacket had infused [her] with some of Vasca's courage' (111). The jacket mediates, in surreal fashion, between the dead Vasca and the living Partnoy, thus rendering it a transitional and melancholy object, as Margaret Gibson defines it. The jacket and the human wearing it now partake of its materiality through a corporeal interface as well: Partnoy *becomes* Vasca through the shared materiality of the jacket.

In *The Farming of Bones* there are numerous instances of the corporeal materiality of witnessing. Haitians who work as labourers in Dominican sugarcane plantations have, literally, the cane inscribed on their bodies. Danticat writing from the point of view of the protagonist Amabelle, says about Sebastien, her lover: 'cane stalks have ripped apart most of the skin on his shiny black face, leaving him with crisscrossed trails of furrowed scars' (1). Another, man, Kongo, has a 'map of scars' on his back (62). Others are equally 'damaged':

> Among the oldest women, one was missing an ear. Two had lost fingers. One had her right cheekbone cracked in half, the result of a run-away machete in the fields. The oldest cane-cutting women were now too sick, too weak, or too crippled to cook or clean in a big house, work the harvest in the cane fields, or return to their old homes in Haiti. (61)

In fact the entire community seems disabled and damaged in some way:

> Clusters of anxious faces peering out from everywhere in the garden, people who looked tired and ill, some with bandages on their shoulders and pieces of clothing acting as slings to hold up their arms. (72)

Such bodies are material witnesses to unequal social processes and injustices in the plantations. Later, bodies such as Amabelle's would also function as testimonies to the genocide and ethnicide perpetrated by the Dominican army. She says of her condition: 'the small bones of my bare feet were grating each other raw' (219), and 'now my flesh was simply a map of scars and bruises, a marred testament' (226). She finds her body losing its cohesion and identity: my 'wider, heavier body slowly fold[ing] towards my feet, as though my bones were being deliberately pulled from their height towards the ground' (267), and 'feel [ing] and liv[ing] my own body's sadness more and more every day' (276). The act of staging her body—involuntary, on occasion, when she observes children staring at her (226)—in the form of inventorying her injuries and disabilities means that Amabelle offers her brutalized body as testimony *in lieu* of a story (as Derrida claims about testimony, 2000: 38).[3]

Heather Hewett reading the corporeal imagery of Danticat's novel writes: 'loss is intensely physical for Amabelle; her body remembers the presence of Sebastien with acute pain' (2006: 131–132). Hewett is citing the following passage:

> His name is Sebastien Onius. Sometimes this is all I know. My back aches now in all those places that he claimed for himself, arches of bare skin that belonged to him, pockets where the flesh remains fragile, seared like unhealed bums where each fallen scab uncovers a deeper wound. (281)

While Hewett is correct in her argument that loss is corporeal for Amabelle, this loss must also be read as a metaphor for the larger loss, of which Sebastien is an instantiation. Her loss marked in corporeal terms gestures at the absence of Sebastien's body *in toto*, with the impossibility of burial, with no indication of his possible grave or mode of death. That is, Amabelle's brutalized body, made visible to the community she lives in, serves as a *memorial* to the dead Sebastien, to the disappeared. In Amabelle's presence, therefore, 'the women wondered out aloud whether Mimi and Sebastien had disappeared forever in the country of death' (237).The body that eyewitnessed its own brutalization and the massacre now *bears witness* to the missing Sebastien, to the hundreds whose bodies were never found. It is a material reminder of those whose materiality is no longer visible. For Amabelle, and others who have been similarly persecuted and bear signs of brutalization, the community is formed, as Lynn Chun Ink proposes, through the 'the shared experience of persecution and loss arising from the massacre' (2004: 804). Thus, it is a community of eyewitnesses and survivors, who together bear witnesses to loss.

Melancholy objects with narrative elaborations in the lives of individuals and bodies functioning as melancholy objects, position the individuals as citizens of a landscape of memories.

Trauma-Memory Citizenship

> Whatever I do, however I find a way to live, I will tell these stories. I have spoken to every person I have encountered these last difficult days ... I speak to these people, and I speak to you because I cannot help it. It gives me strength, almost unbelievable strength, to know that you are there. I covet your eyes, your ears, the collapsible space between us. How blessed are we to have each other? I am alive and you are alive and so we must fill the air with our words. I will fill today, tomorrow, every day until I am taken back to God. I will tell stories to people who will listen and to people who don't want to listen, to people who seek me out and to those who run. All the while I will know that you are there. How can I pretend that you do not exist? It would be almost as impossible as you pretending that I do not exist.

This is Valentino Achak Deng's resolution at the very end—it is the last paragraph of the novel—of *What is the What* (535). Deng, who has thus far carried on his 'conversation' (in his head) with the users of the gym in which he works, the boy who holds him hostage in his own home and assorted others, sees himself as constituting an audience through his storytelling.

The articulation of witnessing in the form of memories, stories and the victim-body (as the material articulation of a process) constitute a publics.[4] The transmission, inheritance and sharing of memory as a defining feature of identity, individual and communitarian, is a common theme in the HR novel, and demonstrates the ruins of a social order *in the present* due to the persistent presence of this memory. Memory constitutes the very world in which the individual is embedded. However, this is a set of memories of being once dehumanized, of pain, that return, to once again destroy the possibility of a coherent self.

Almost every HR text insists that storytelling and the recall of traumatic memories is essential—for reconciliation and forgiveness, for a better understanding of history and for different imaginings of the nation. HR novels depict traumatic memories as constitutive of the individual's life, and very often the community's identity, in the present. In HR novels unsustainable ecosystems inimical to life are not always described as real settings. Rather, these are given to us in the form of thoughts and memories, visions and ideas, and of course stories, suggestive of an ecosystem existing within the minds of the people even though the materiality of that past age has been erased. The HR novel suggests that memories are material and constitute the survivors in particular ways, continuing to inform their subjectivities.

The photographs of the missing carried by the Mothers at the Plaza de Mayo in *Imagining Argentina* become the symbolic reference point of this ecosystem. Allende writes in *Of Love and Shadows*: 'hundreds of people held a sit-in in the street in front of the Vicariate, displaying photographs of their missing loved ones, whispering, where are they? Where are they?' (237). The questions indicate not only the epistemological uncertainty around individuals but also the attempt to frame loss and memories of that loss within an interrogation of the system that *produced* that loss. The missing son in *Red Dust*, the unidentified body in *Anil's Ghost* and *Under the Bone*, Raami's missing father in *In the Shadow of the Banyan*, the missing Sebastien in *The Farming of Bones* are examples of a former disappearance that continues to define the family's or a community's present. The individual remains situated in this historical past of tortures, disappearances and incarceration. By bringing up the historical and personal pasts, they blur the private/public distinction as well.

Subjects in these novels are constituted by their individual and collective memories: individuals participate in larger, communitarian, social and even national projects of recall, thus suggesting a 'memory citizenship'

(Rothberg and Yildiz 2011). That is, there is no escape from memories of the events that have happened to/been done to their bodies and minds. This is particularly true of novels set in post-Apartheid South Africa, such as Gillian Slovo's *Red Dust*, J.M. Coetzee's *Disgrace* and Achmat Dangor's *Bitter Fruit*, where coming to terms with the brutal history of the country means keeping memories of the period alive, and often coming face to face with ghosts from the past. The project of remembering, as documented in novels dealing with the TRCs, is a fraught one, and the state, victims and those mediating processes of justice are all stake-holders in what is remembered, and how. At this point, I shall only deal with the trauma of individuals whose lives are caught up in the process of remembering—collective memory, especially of genocides, will figure in the later chapter.

In HR texts the enunciation of trauma initiates a membership into what may be thought of as *trauma*-memory citizenship, and constitutes the political subjectification of the victim-witness. Regimes of truth-telling that call for a *trauma*-memory citizenship are organized around two key axes. First, in Gil Eyal's reading, 'memory is the guarantor of *identity* and maintains it through time—it is the mechanism of *retention* responsible for the experience of being a selfsame individual moving through time' (2004: 7, emphasis in original). In many cases 'this injunction to remember meant that the characteristic *mnemonic operation* of the … will to memory was the recovery of traces of national existence, traces lost, forgotten, censored or falsified' (14, emphasis in original), and is essentially a collective memory project. Thus in *The Farming of Bones* Father Romain preaching to the Haitians, working as labourers, in the Dominican Republic 'often reminded them everyone of common ties: language, foods, history, carnival, songs, tales, and prayers'. Father Romain's 'creed was one of memory—how remembering—though sometimes painful—can make you strong' (73).Together, to adapt Eyal's words, 'they comprised the continuity of national existence' (15).

Second, 'memory plays a role in over-coming psychic *trauma* and the processes of dissociation it sets in motion' so that, it is assumed, 'individuals are healed by remembering that which was repressed' (Eyal7, emphasis in original). Together these axes constitute what Eyal calls the 'will to memory'. In HR texts, the second dimension of the will to memory is more pronounced, but always qualified due to an anxiety regarding the efficacy of the 'healing'.[5]

The memory citizenship in all these novels is a trauma-memory citizenship. Most novels are entirely devoted to the theme of cultural memory and the violence of its retrieval (Ondaatje's *Anil's Ghost*, Anne-christined' Adesky's *Under the Bone*, Slovo's *Red Dust*). The HR novel's portrayal of trauma-memory citizenship, I propose, is the documentation of a legacy but a legacy that demands, at once, visitation and forgetting. In *Anil's Ghost*, therefore, Anil's effort is to prevent the complete obliteration of Sri Lanka's memory of ethnicide and mass killings: she literally 'unburies' them in her job as a forensic anthropologist.

Alex Mpondo in Slovo's *Red Dust*, face to face with Dirk Hendricks, the policeman who tortured him in the apartheid era, notes the expression of the 'torturer who had haunted his life', even in the present (183–184). Individuals displaced from Haiti seek to leave 'imprints of themselves in each other's memory', writes Danticat in *The Farming of Bones* (72–73).

In *Bitter Fruit* Silas Ali's encounter with the now retired policeman Du Boise ensures that his and his wife Lydia's 'free' and democratic present is still shackled to their past: Lydia had been raped by Du Boise. Their son Mike ponders on the nature of historical memory:

> Yet, it [the term historical memory] has an air of inevitability, solemn and compelling ... It explains everything, the violence periodically sweeping the country, the crime rate, even the strange "upsurge" of brutality against women. It is as if history has a remembering process of its own, one that gives life to its imaginary monsters. Now his mother and father have received a visitation from that dark past. (32)

The past—of arrests, torture, executions, disappearances—remains the ecosystem in the present as well. If the law then was ineffective, in the age of apartheid, it remains ineffective now too: 'nothing in her life would have changed, nothing in any of their lives would change because of a public confession of pain suffered. Because nothing could be undone,' thinks Lydia about appearing before the TRC and submitting her petition about being raped (156). Thus, in *Red Dust*, the Commission investigating the Apartheid atrocities does not effect any reconciliation: on the contrary it retains the mysteries of the disappeared people and continues to inform the lives of the people alive in the present.

The novel is generically suited to this task of demonstrating repetition, doubling and reiteration of a past ecosystem in the *present*. The new is simply an instance wherein memories break open, thanks to continued disappearances (*Imagining Argentina*, *Anil's Ghost*) and institutional mechanisms devoted to 'reconciling' (with) the past, at least in people's minds (David Park's *The Truth Commissioner*, Slovo's *Red Dust*). In Paul Gready's terms:

> the webs of containment that have formed through intersecting political and personal silences, secrets, denials, and forgettings, around multiple layers of pain and betrayal, are broken open. Or more accurately they are reformulated alongside memory and confession as the narrative unfolds, new layers added on old. (2009: 169)

Given the fact that the TRC seeks to revisit an old injury, novels like David Park's *The Truth Commissioner* and Gillian Slovo's *Red Dust* offer us an interesting insight into the TRC's memory cultures.

These novels critique the TRC fantasy where the subject who has already been reduced, in the course of torture, into a dehumanized, abject figure is now asked to publicly admit to this dehumanization, almost as though her/his subjectivity might be somehow restored (reconciled) afterwards. The participation in the memory citizenship project wherein their memories are subsumed into a national cultural text or memory also calls for a balance between their singular subjective response and an intersubjectivity with other such victims. Thus, in *Man of Bone*, the social worker at the therapy session asks people to narrate their experiences. And one of those present men admits to being raped. The episode ends:

> The social worker leans in toward Linga. "How did that make you feel?" she asks again.
>
> "Very bad," he says.
>
> She writes that down on her paper, as if somehow he has told her something she didn't know. (103)

Cumyn here is pointing to the sheer callousness in the process of documenting victim-experiences, forcing them to recall their traumas and especially their emotional states during their experiences. Coetzee notes this crisis in storytelling by comparing it to torture itself in *Waiting for the Barbarians.* The Magistrate screams at the barbarian girl: "What did they do to you? ... Why don't you want to tell me? ... Tell me ... don't make a mystery of it" (34). As Maria Lopez notes: 'there is, throughout Coetzee's novels, a concern with verbal penetration: with the attempt, on the part of one character, to appropriate the story or inner secret of another character' (2010: 928). We see this anxiety around narrative appropriations in Danticat's *Farming of Bones* as well. Here two Dominican priests 'listen and mark down testimonials' of the Santiago slaughter (246). Yves, uncertain of the purpose of this witness-narrative collection, comments to Amabelle:

> they're collecting tales for newspapers and radio men. The Generalissimo has found ways to buy and sell the ones here … You tell the story, and then it's retold as they wish, written in words you do not understand, in a language that is theirs, not yours. (246)

Further, these novels propose that retelling the accounts of their dehumanization and debasement is an extension or repetition of the trauma. Finally, revisiting the trauma, often with the perpetrator sitting across the table/room in the TRC hearing, poses its own set of dangers to the 'recovered' subject. Together, these are violent acts for, as Aryn Bartley phrases it:

> It asks us to see the process of compiling public narrations into a larger national history as participating in forms of narrative or discursive violence, and the public context of this kind of storytelling as producing its own material dangers. (2009: 105)

The demand to offer up to the public the process through which one's subjectivity had been eroded is a violent act, and this violence of the subject world informs the 'recovery' process of individuals in many cultures such as Argentina, Chile and South Africa. This violence of officially demanded and allegedly recuperative memory does not institute the subject of torture as a repaired or reconciled subject in the contemporary HR novel. Rather, it locks them back into that past. Memory citizenship that ought to define them as having 'moved on' renders them tethered to their pasts. Thus for Silas in *Bitter Fruit*, what Du Boise had done was 'a faded moon of a memory that only occasionally intruded into his everyday consciousness' (4), but the encounter with the old policeman, which he narrates to Lydia, opens up the wounds of memory.

That is, the unmaking of the subject world inaugurated, as studied in Chap. 1, through the emplacement of individuals in horrific situations, is now the effect of a reiteration of the memory of the military regime, Apartheid or a tyrannical past. The subject world is unmade because the once-unmade subject remains embedded in that past, and so the present world is unmade by and through memories. The HR novel is deeply critical of memory citizenships where these subjects remain handcuffed to their terrible histories due to the official process of recounting them.

Trauma-memory citizenship is therefore open to more than just the tortured themselves: it allows family members, acquaintances, friends and associates to participate in the citizenship project. This could be through the sharing of grief, through witnessing the torture of the other or through the circulation of stories about tortures, in forms like the TRCs. In the case of the disappeared, for instance, a cloak of secrecy and attendant rumours envelops the community in *Red Dust*, *Imagining Argentina* and *Anil's Ghost*. Reinhold Görling notes 'a curious tension between secrecy and revelation peculiar to torture. It takes place in cellars and camps fenced with barbed wire, but it is also exhibited: as rumour, as picture' (66). In *Anil's Ghost*, Ondtaaje captures this unnerving haunting, of ghosting, that anchors a community: 'Mass disappearances at Suriyakanda, reports of mass graves at Ankumbura, mass graves at Akmeemana. Half the world, it felt, was being buried, the truth hidden by fear, while the past revealed itself in the light of a burning rhododendron bush' (156).

One can think of this subject world of the present constituted by the recalled past as an inverted subject world detrimental to the social ontology of the survivor. If the regime had once destroyed the subject embedded in the system of tyranny, culture of fear or the physical space of the prison, the present subject world constituted by memories, stories and TRCs is equally destructive.

It is no longer corporeal vulnerability (in terms of the body's openness to pain and suffering) but the institutional mechanisms of making formerly experienced pain available as a public spectacle in terms of processes like courts and TRCs that the HR novel depicts. The public detailing of memories that is directed at 'reconciliation' actually undoes the world the tortured subject carefully puts back after the event. Thus Lucy in *Disgrace* calls her rape a 'purely private matter' (112). And Lydia in Dangor's *Bitter Fruit* absolutely refuses to talk about her rape to the police or even to her family. This refusal to talk about their tortures in TRCs and courts of law might be seen as efforts to retain the personal nature of their traumatic memory.

In other cases, fiction writers suggest that the world itself should be brought into the ambit of trauma-memory citizenship so that everybody becomes witness to the horror. This theme of the world bearing witness to the events in such situations is manifest in the form of an emphasis on language, narrative, on storytelling and on documentation. In many cases it is the breakdown of language itself that signals the impossibility of narrating what happened and the necessity of finding a language in order to do so. In Lawrence Thornton's *Naming the Spirits* (1996) the sole survivor of a massacre during the Dirty War in Argentina has lost her capacity for language but eventually delivers the names of the disappeared and massacred to the public. Michael Ondaatje's *Anil's Ghost*, in addition to underscoring the language of forensics (to decipher the identity of the genocides) concludes with the voice of Sarath, who has now been taken away for torture and certain execution, emanating from a cassette clandestinely smuggled inside the skeleton they were examining. Sarath offers evidence of the state's role in the 'production' of this particular death. In Rivabella's *Requiem for a Woman's Soul* Susana writes in pain and in practically indecipherable script (with blood and faeces on scraps of tissue and toilet paper) that Father Antonio, the recipient of these texts, has to carefully interpret and translate. Eventually, Antonio himself is driven to insanity and the novel concludes with him mumbling 'unintelligible words' (Epilogue). In *Breaking the Tongue* Ling-li, now dead, 'calls' Claude in his dream and asks him to return to prison so that he might record the manner in which she was tortured: 'If you won't remember and record this, who will? This is how our history starts and is transmitted. Witness and transmission of Story' (480). In this dream he 'sees' Ling-li being tortured, as she calls out to him, not to help her but to record 'their faces, height, distinguishing features. Every bit to erase their anonymity' (481). Claude stands *in the place of* the recorder, the witness and the memoir. And Ling-li 'reads' what he has recorded in his mind (482). In *Imagining Argentina* Carlos is able to 'see' in his visions the events that befall the disappeared—and he reveals these visions in the form of narratives to the families of the disappeared. Lydia in *Bitter Fruit* has recorded the event of rape in a journal. In *Man of Bone* Burridge, when finally freed and recovering, tries to kill himself: the social worker who arrives at the scene as he is being taken away in an ambulance asks: 'And how did it feel when they did that? What did they do next? Then what?' thus asking for a narrative (186). The American official also wants to know. Soon after the rescue he meets Burridge to say: 'What we want to know, Bill, is what they did to you' (171). The demand here, I propose, functions at two levels: to verify that Bill remains the same person as he was before (given especially that he was a diplomat and thus a supposedly 'immune' representative of his nation) and asking him to bear witness to the conditions—civil war, local militia, and so on—that *produced* his torture. It is not enough that he presents his tortured body, apparently. When Burridge finally slashes his wrist in a suicide attempt it becomes therefore an act of agency in determining his end-of-life in the face of demands that he continue, and continue to bring his memory to the public.

The storytelling component of these novels gestures at the *necessity* to enter the torture chamber, via the stories, in order to see the institutional mechanisms—the socio-institutional precariousness—that enabled torture. Witnessing is no longer restricted to what the survivors saw but expanded to include the world in the form of the dark archives. It cannot be simply in terms of numbers for, as Wislawa Szymborska puts it in her 'Hunger Camp at Jasło',

> history counts its skeletons in round numbers
> A thousand and one remain a thousand
> as though the one had never existed.
> (in Forché 459)

If individual stories are erased in favour of numerical inventorying, suggests the poem, then it simply effaces and erases the individual from history. In other cases there is song that survives, as in Heberto Padilla's 'Song of the Juggler', which opens with: 'there's a battle/between your orders and my songs' and ends with:

> General, I can't destroy your fleets or your tanks
> And I don't know how long this war will last
> But every night one of your orders dies without
> being followed,
> and, undefeated, one of my song survives.
> (In Forché 603)

Trauma-memory citizenship entails individualized memories and the circulation of individual stories.

This participation in the trauma-memory citizenship in the form of the circulation of letters, memoirs and stories of their and others' experiences that the HR torture novel compiles is a key component of invigorating the task of language itself, and of spreading the task of witnessing amongst the world so that larger numbers of readers are made aware of institutional mechanisms, state collusion and power structures that make torture possible. Even though classified as fictional reconstructions, these texts construct narrative societies. Emplacement is not only about the participation in a trauma-memory citizenship but the possibility of having an audience to tell the traumatic story to.

Trauma-memory citizenship is extremely traumatic for the survivors and victims as they recall their abject emplacement and abject embodiment: Alex Mpondo in *Red Dust* is an instance, and the refusal of Lucy (*Disgrace*) and Lydia (*Bitter Fruit*) to speak of their violations need to be read as the avoidance of the trauma of *repetition*. James Dawes therefore writes of 'the way the Commission caused some survivors to relive their original traumatic helplessness—became, itself, a doubling of this repetition' (2007: 183).

The Truth Commissioner states this, the first dimension of the will to memory—the rebuilding of an identity for the community through memory—explicitly in the words of Henry Stanfield about the process of TRCs and the accompanying iteration of memories, collective and individual:

> We also need to remember that we're working in a society that has been deeply divided for thousands of years. This is probably the most challenging thing it's ever been asked to do and sometimes it's going to falter and it's going to get frightened but if we can carry it off, then it's the most important step this community can possibly take toward lasting healing. (244–245)

Given the fact that this little speech comes the day after an old woman seeks to stab her husband's killer in the TRC precincts, Stanfield's rhetoric does appear awkward and platitudinous at best. Stanfield's assumption is a manifestation of the *crisis* of memory the TRC engenders.

Eyal points out when defining the 'crisis of memory', the investment in memory as ensuring continuity of identity produces too *much* memory, and the investment in memory as helping overcome trauma produces too *little* memory: the 'investment of memory with the function of overcoming trauma and protecting society from repetition generates the sense of an unstable memory, undermined from within and continuously swinging between fact, fantasy and falsity' (7). Thus *The Truth Commissioner* opens with the destruction of records indicating the attempt to undermine the modes of memory-making in the TRC's processes (46–49). In *The Truth Commissioner* Stanfield expects the nation to attain, or retain, a sense of its identity in the process of recounting, even when the identity itself, as he admits, is 'deeply divided'. There is far *too much* memory of pre-existing tensions and violence that haunts all members of the society for the recounting to effect a simple reconciliation and forgiveness. Further, officially, there is an attempt to retain *very little* memory of the terrors visited upon the people. In *The Farming of Bones*, 'the Justice of the Peace recording the testimonials from Haitian survivors, simply stops coming one day: 'the justice of the peace had already gone away when no one was looking' and the head sergeant announces that 'there would be no more testimonials taken' (235). Memories, Raami is instructed in *In the Shadow of the Banyan*, 'make you weak … for memory is sickness' (188). And her mother explicitly cautions her that their family's identity—as Royals—is not to be revealed through an articulation of her, Raami's, memory: 'However you loved your papa, Raami, you must learn to keep his memory to yourself' (188).

Memory citizenship's paradox—its potential to turn into trauma-memory citizenship through the institutionalized recall—is that abjection is now brought back, first into discourse and then materially. In *Red Dust* Alex Mpondo's hands shake badly when in the precincts of the TRC (201). On one occasion he leaves the TRC, goes out and throws up as he recalls his tortures:

> The dirt under Dirk Hendricks' nails … Sounds … those screams building up, battering his ears, the terror gripping him so tightly … then screaming himself until they came and held him down. (133)

Slovo depicts a visceral response to the *discursive* recounting of the injuries he suffered in prison. Thornton in *Imagining Argentina* describes the trial of the generals and the response of the people when they hear the account of the events: 'I saw their eyes filling the blood and terror of memory' (212). Paul Sweetbread breaks down in tears recounting his own role in the massacres in *The Persistence of Memory* (261).

Witnessing and Political Subjectification

If subjectivity is constituted through witnessing, as Kelly Oliver has argued and this chapter has examined in the case of HR texts, then structures of testimonial recounting and testamentary enunciation of memories of torture produce specific forms of political subjectification. The anthropologist Didier Fassin defines political subjectification as 'the advent of subjects and subjectivities onto a political scene … [these subjects] are figures that enable individuals to be described (by others) and identified (by themselves) in the public arena' (533).Thus 'in the political arena, trauma produces the suffering being just as humanitarianism produces the victim' (533). HR texts move from abject subjects of torture and oppression to witnessing subjects who, in the process of recounting their nightmarish experiences, insert themselves into politically charged memories of the land, processes such as the TRCs, political campaigns, among others. Several HR texts call into question processes such as trials and TRCs for the kind of political subjectification they either return victims to or create anew. HR texts may be organized into two categories around their theme of political subjectivity emerging from trauma-memory citizenship.[6]

In the first category is a set of HR texts wherein political subjectivity is often altered so that rather than come to terms with their pasts—reconciliation—they look at an uncertain future.

After the psychiatrist has cast an interrogative over his supposed total recall talent, Paul Sweetbread in *The Persistence of Memory* thinks of how his own lawyer (Dini) has, by cross-examining the psychiatrist, undermined his, Sweetbread's, confidence in himself:

> She [Dini] thinks she has helped me by undercutting Dr Vish's testimony. Yet I need only look at him and I am back in his office, a small child attentive to the only adult who seems aware of the enormous burden that the child's memory imposes ... I fear that Dini has well-meaningly sliced through one more guy-line that holds my unruly zeppelin still tethered to the ground. (261)

Sweetbread's mental strength is beginning to give way and each analysis (cross-examination) of his attitudes, memories and emotional make-up in the TRC undermines him just that much more. The infantilizing trope that we see in the above passage is the erasure of his political subjectivity as witness. The events in the TRC remind him of the role he himself, as a white soldier in the army, played during the war. The impossibility of being a mere bystander and therefore the imminent participation in the horrors the army chooses to perpetrate constitute Sweetbread's political subjectivity as a perpetrator. Lyddie tells him: '"I hate that look that says, *I don't like this, but I'm not going to get involved.* You're part of this, old son, like it or not. So now you know"' (140, emphasis in original). This comment comes after Lyddie has ascribed responsibility and ethical behaviour to Sweetbread, with the full awareness that Sweetbread cannot use either:

> You disapproved of my actions in that kaffir kraal, nee? So what did you do about it? ... You think your silent objection means you have no responsibility. All you had to do was say *Stop it!* and that's what I would have done (137, emphasis in original)

Lyddie is suggesting that having been eyewitness to his, Lyddie's, horrific actions (of immersing a native chief's infant in a barrel of water, 135–136), Sweetbread was morally bound to *stop* Lyddie. His later comment then builds on this attribution of moral responsibility (to Sweetbread) in order to point out that, by not stopping Lyddie Sweetbread had effectively demonstrated his own complicity and participation as a perpetrator. This is Sweetbread's political subjectivity, brought on by his function as a non-objecting witness.[7]

Alex Mpondo's deposition in *Red Dust* positions him as the victim of Pieter Muller's and Dirk Hendricks' racialized torture, although Hendricks gets his Amnesty approved. Mpondo, however, is a Member of Parliament. Dirk Hendricks' thoughts about Mpondo towards the end of the novel are as follows: 'Let her pass it [her unease that Hendricks lied about when Mpondo broke—before or after Steve's death] on to Mpondo in his new life with his MP's salary and his friends in high places. Let him live with the knowledge that he had killed his friend' (336). Mpondo himself recognizes that his life after torture, and as a respected member of the community, as freedom-fighter, has unravelled as a result of the return to the political subjectivity constructed in the TRC's frame. He thinks: 'It was such a struggle to free myself from that man's clutches ... I won't be his victim again ... I am not and I will not be, their victim'. But this political subjectification is not merely the result of the psychological play Hendricks indulges in: he had indicted Mpondo in the TRC and thus constructed a political subjectivity for Mpondo within the public arena. Mpondo would be the man who broke under torture and betrayed his friend and comrade. That is, Mpondo's public (TRC) arraignment as *betrayer* by Hendricks rearranges his political subjectivity.

In *Imagining Argentina* the survivors of the 'disappeared' and the victims of torture come to the trial and scream '*Nunca más*! [never again]' (212–213) after testifying against the generals. The process of the trial and their participatory presence in it as witnesses constructs them as victims-survivors of the regime. Having discovered that his father is a mass-murderer, Cornelius in *Murambi* decides that 'it was his duty to get as close as he could to all suffering' ('Cornelius'). Cornelius' political subjectification is a mixture of redemption on behalf of his father and compensation—for having been away all these years. Michael in *Bitter Fruit* kills DuBoise, the man who raped his mother—he is the son of this rape—and then decides to take his chances with life elsewhere: in Islam, specifically. Michael's political subjectification is not the result of his public witnessing but his participation, indirectly, in the history of his family via his mother's diary. As the progeny of interracial rape, his political subjectification is, in a sense, fixed for life, and his murderous acts are modes to escape being trapped by this subjectivity and find his own elsewhere.

A second category of HR texts exists where there is a conscious decision on the part of the victim-witness *not* to attain a measure of political subjectification through public admissions of witnessing. Thus Lucy in *Disgrace* refuses to lodge a complaint about her rape. Yet, her decision 'to start at ground level' with 'nothing ... No cards, no weapons, no property, no rights, no dignity' (205) is the acceptance of a political subjectivity engendered not by *her* active participation in witnessing but others—her rapists—who had witnessed her humiliation and her eventual quiescence. Lydia of *Bitter Fruit*, like *Disgrace's* Lucy, refuses to go public about her rape. Dangor's scepticism about the nature of political subjectivity produced by trauma-memory citizenship and witnessing is stated unambiguously:

> It would not have helped her to appear before the Commission, even at a closed hearing. The offer had been made, a special session on abused women ... Nothing in her life would have changed, nothing in any of their lives would change because of a public confession of pain suffered. Because nothing could be undone, you could not withdraw a rape, it was an irrevocable act ... it could not be withdrawn, not by an act of remorse or vengeance, not even by justice. (155–156)

The humiliation, recognition, suspicion around figures like Lucy or Michael constitute them as political subjects, of subjects who bear witness to something that they refuse to talk about. Under threat of assassination for her role in revealing the military's excesses, Irene in *Of Love and Shadows* is forced to flee her country. The novel ends with her sobbing at the border she is about to cross, into another country and safety: 'she thought of the magnitude of her loss ... she would never hear her language spoken as she loved it ... she was not only losing Rosa, her mother, her work, and her past. She was losing her homeland' (297). The process of ensuring justice for the families of the disappeared—which is what brings Irene to the brink of her execution by the state—has resulted in her utter and complete displacement.

Thus the HR novel treats abjection as part of a process of political subjectification, whether the victims bear public witness to this abjection or not. Abject emplacements and embodiment, especially when recalled in formal, institutionalized settings, continue to have the power to alter and define their political subjectivity.

Notes

1. I am not addressing the question of the empathic *listener* to or *reader* of the trauma narrative here. Rather I am interested in one victim being an empathic witness to another's suffering. For empathic listening as integral to the project of trauma narratives and their telling see Felman and Laub (1992). Critics like Dominic LaCapra have argued that a certain 'vicarious victimhood' arises out of identification with the victim (1999: 699).
2. Brenda Carr Vellino proposes that we think in terms of a witness continuum, made or primary, secondary and tertiary witnesses, from writing in the aftermath of first-hand experiences (primary witnesses) to those who did not experience the events but felt compelled to respond to (secondary witnesses) and finally poems in which 'speakers … stand as avatars for the mediated position of readers as tertiary witnesses, who are also summoned to extend the chain of witnessing response to the provisional human rights subjects of the poems' (2016: 150).
3. Of bones bearing witnesses to genocide and massacres, there are several examples, from the unidentified skeleton in *Anil's Ghost* to the heap of skeletons in *Murambi* and the bones of the 'martyrs' as the victims are called in *Sandcastle Girls*. But in this present reading I am looking at living bodies and material objects as witnesses.
4. Even unshared, memory could also *be* an individual's identity. For instance, in *Anil's Ghost* Anil encounters a woman in Guatemala who has lost both her husband and her brother. The woman sits in an open excavation site that serves as a communal unmarked grave, sitting with

> her legs under her as if in formal prayer … There are no words Anil knows that can describe, even for just herself, the woman's face. But the grief of love in that shoulder she will not forget, still remembers. (5–6)

The woman's entire identity is defined by the memory of her loved, and missing, ones. Anil herself is transfixed by the *sight* of the mourning woman: the woman mourns in the absence of the bodies.

5. 'Healing', incidentally, was a term often associated with the TRC processes. In Park's *The Truth Commissioner*, he writes of Henry Stanfield: 'he hears the word healing so often that he wants to stand up and shout that perhaps they should have employed doctors instead of representatives of the law' (49).
6. My reading of these texts is more in tune with Aryn Bartley's argument about TRC-based texts. Bartley writes:

   > [These novels urge us] to rethink not the legitimacy of public storytelling, but rather its processes and contexts ... Recognizing the perhaps unavoidable violence of national storytelling ... might help produce a vision of community that allows for conflict and difference, a depiction of the public sphere that acknowledges its dangers, and an even more complex conceptualization of history and narration. (2009: 123–124)

7. Paul Gready reading this scene writes: 'as witness and combatant he can no longer remain a mere bystander, or expect others to do his dirty work for him' (2009: 172). But this is not an adequate interpretation if we take the two Lyddie comments together, for those seem to clearly construct Sweetbread as a silent witness and therefore, implicitly, an acquiescent participant.

Bibliography

Bartley, Aryn. 2009. The Violence of the Present: *David's Story* and the Truth and Reconciliation Commission. *Comparative Literature Studies* 46(1): 103–124.

Berlant, Lauren. 2004. Introduction: Compassion (and Withholding), In *Compassion: The Culture and Politics of an Emotion,* ed. Berlant, 1–13. New York: Routledge.

———. 2009. *Frames of War: When is Life Grievable?* London: Verso.

Dawes, James. 2007. *That the World May Know: Bearing Witness to Atrocity.* Cambridge, MA: Harvard University Press.

Eaglestone, Robert. 2008. "You Would Not Add to My Suffering If You Knew What I Have Seen": Holocaust Testimony and Contemporary African Trauma Literature. *Studies in the Novel* 40(1–2): 72–85.

Eyal, Gil. 2004. Identity and Trauma: Two Forms of the Will to Memory. *History and Memory* 16(1): 5–36.

Felman, Shoshana and Dori Laub. 1992. *Testimony: Crises of Witnessing in Literature, Psychoanalysis, and History*. New York: Routledge.

Gibson, Margaret. 2004. Melancholy Objects. *Mortality* 9(4): 285–299.

Gready, Paul. 2009. Novel Truths: Literature and Truth Commissions. *Comparative Literature Studies* 46(1): 156–176.

Hewett, Heather. 2006. At the Crossroads: Disability and Trauma in *The Farming of Bones*. *Melus* 31(3): 123–144.

Ink, Lynn Chun. 2004. Remaking Identity, Unmaking Nation: Historical Recovery and the Reconstruction of Community in *In the Time of the Butterflies* and *The Farming of Bones*. *Callaloo* 27(3): 788–807.

Keen, Suzanne. 2007. *Empathy and the Novel*. New York: Oxford University Press.

LaCapra, Dominic. 1999. Trauma, Absence, Loss. *Critical Inquiry* 25(4): 696–727.

———. 2001. *Writing History, Writing Trauma*. Baltimore: Johns Hopkins University Press.

Morris, Rosalind C. 2011. In the Name of Trauma: Notes on Testimony, Truth Telling and the Secret of Literature in South Africa. *Comparative Literature Studies* 48(3): 389–416.

Oliver, Kelly. 2001. *Witnessing: Beyond Recognition*. Minneapolis: Minnesota University Press.

Razinsky, Liran. 2010. Not the Witness We Wished For: Testimony in Jonathan Littell's *Kindly Ones*. *Modern Language Quarterly* 71(2): 175–196.

Rothberg, Michael, and Yasemin Yildiz. 2011. Memory Citizenship: Migrant Archives of Holocaust Remembrance in Contemporary Germany. *Parallax* 17(4): 32–48.

Thornton, Lawrence. 1996. *Naming the Spirits*. New York: Bantam.

Vellino, Brenda Carr. 2016. Beyond the Trauma Aesthetic: The Cultural Work of Human Rights Witness Poetries. In *The Routledge Companion to Literature and Human Rights*, ed. Sophia McClennen, and Alexandra Schultheis Moore, 148–158. New York: Routledge.

CHAPTER 4

Collectives

Thus far the chapters have examined the individual human subject of Human Rights as emplaced, embodied and witnessing. HR literature also pays considerable attention to collectives, especially novels that concern themselves with ethnic cleansing, genocidal violence and massacres. In the preceding chapters I dealt with the genocidal imaginary that constructs situations wherein torture, executions and incarcerations are rendered possible. I now extend this line of thought in order to examine how collectives are represented in novels that foreground the violation of Human Rights.

HR texts that focus on individual sufferings also at several points in the narrative pay attention to *social* suffering. Social suffering 'results from what political, economic, and institutional power does to people and, reciprocally, from how these forms of power themselves influence responses to social problems' (Kleinman et al. 1997). It thus proceeds from the political, economic, cultural and social conditions in which individuals are placed. HR texts portray social suffering not only in terms of massacres and mass exterminations but also 'expose [life] to death', to borrow Achille Mbembe's phrasing (2003: 12). This 'exposing' life to death could be in terms of everyday life lived under constant sniper fire (*The Cellist of Sarajevo*), deliberate exposure of entire groups of people to inclement weather and denial of food and water (as happens to the Armenians in *Sandcastle Girls*), raids and random arrests (*Imagining Argentina*, *Of Love and Shadows*), starvation and inadequate safety (*In*

P.K. Nayar, *Human Rights and Literature*,
DOI 10.1057/978-1-137-50432-6_4

the Shadow of the Banyan), horrific working conditions (*The Farming of Bones*), among others.

Detailing social suffering, such texts portray fragile communities (made up of, certainly, vulnerable individuals) that exist on the margins, or at risk of obliteration through prolonged deprivation. The texts locate these communities within a trauma-scape, on what anthropologist Nancy Scheper-Hughes presciently terms a 'genocide continuum'. Elaborating this idea, she writes:

> I have suggested a genocide continuum … made up of a multitude of "small wars and invisible genocides" conducted in the normative social spaces of public schools, clinics, emergency rooms, hospital wards, nursing homes, court rooms, prisons, detention centers, and public morgues. The continuum refers to the human capacity to reduce others to nonpersons, to monsters, or to things that give structure, meaning, and rationale to everyday practices of violence. It is essential that we recognize in our species (and in ourselves) *a genocidal capacity* and that we exercise a defensive hypervigilance, a hypersensitivity to the less dramatic, *permitted,* everyday acts of violence that make participation (under other conditions) in genocidal acts possible, perhaps more easy than we would like to know. I would include all expressions of social exclusion, dehumanization, depersonalization, pseudospeciation, and reification that normalize atrocious behavior and violence toward others. (2002: 369, emphasis in original)

HR texts clearly point to the existence of such a genocide continuum where specific groups of people are in a constantly embattled state, facing everyday violence, discrimination and exclusion. The genocidal continuum helps mobilize people to participate in the genocidal campaign, and it is from this genocide continuum that structures of extermination emerge. The genocide continuum finds its expression in HR texts in three specific forms: the making of zones of indistinction, cultures of mourning and counterpublics. The first two are manifestations of the genocide continuum wherein lives blur into death. The third marks a *response* to the genocide continuum in when counterpublics come into being as a result of collective memory-making at national or communitarian level.

Zones of Indistinction

The genocide continuum ensures that groups and communities are emplaced within structures wherein their lives border on death. These structures—detention centres, refugee camps, prisons, torture cells—are spaces where everyday life is on the verge of death, where life is exposed to death on a regular basis. Clearly, the genocide continuum has more to do with everyday life and 'normalized' violence rather than exceptional circumstances so that the extreme coexists with the everyday for a great many individuals. As Scheper-Hughes' definition emphasizes, the continuum has to do with how atrocity is permitted, gets normalized and even expected (as is the case with, say, the treatment of Armenians by Turks in *Sandcastle Girls*). The genocide continuum ensures that a 'zone of indistinction' (Agamben 1998) is created within which the everyday lives of some people slide and veer towards death. In the zone of indistinction legality and illegality, legitimate interrogative modes and torture, the rule of law and its suspension and finally life and death are blurred. Legal citizens are taken into this zone, illegally tortured until they admit to 'criminal' or 'treasonous' acts that then condemn them to the category of 'outlaws'. Yet, it is not necessarily the prison or the camp in which such zones are constructed: the zone of indistinction is any place wherein, due to the genocide continuum, the subjects are poised to lose their subjectivity. Citizenship therefore is blurred into 'bare life' in the zone of indistinction. Outside, the family members and community do not know with any degree of certainty whether the ones taken away—'disappeared'—are alive or dead.

HR texts map these zones of indistinction, geographical and social spaces of life, blurring into death in three distinct but not unrelated modes.

Landscapes of Disappearance

'The country existed in a rocking selfburying motion. The disappearance of schoolboys, the death of lawyers by torture, the abduction of bodies from the Hokandara mass grave,' Ondaatje writes in *Anil's Ghost* (157). Sarath tells Anil:

> There was only one thing worse [than having family members killed]. That was when a family member disappeared and there was no sighting or evidence of his existence or death. In 1989, forty-six students attending school in Ratnapura disappeared, and some of the staff who worked there disappeared. (184–185)

Horst Bienek in 'Exodus' writes:

> They drove us out
> On nights when moons died,
> And around us sprouted
> A forest of hostile bayonets.
>
> (In Forché 469)

The landscape is populated by exiles, the dead and the dying. The image of 'sprouting', traditionally associated with growth and life here serves to symbolize a landscape of death. In Claribel Alegria's 'We Were Three' the speaker complains: 'my dead wait/at every corner' and even the 'grillwork of balconies' becomes the 'filmed mirror of my dead' (in Forché 588). Even when the streets are empty, the speaker says, the 'dead wink' at her/him (589).

In Allende's *Of Love and Shadows* the protagonists arrive at an old, abandoned mine in a 'wild and lonely landscape' (191). Their view of the space not only anthropomorphs the landscape, it also conveys a topographical symbolism of large-scale suffering: 'the entrance to the mine drilled in the mountainside looked like a mouth shouting a silent scream … Loneliness had settled in to stay, obscuring marks of a trail or any memory of life' (192). Minoli Salgado describing sites such as the above writes:

> Here cartography is determined by ethical rather than geographical coordinates: truth or material facts are suppressed to the point of invisibility and reality is marked by the bodies of the disappeared—a landscape, it could be said, marked by the truth of disappearance and the disappearance of truth. (2013: 210)

Landscapes of disappearance are burial sites where the unsavoury truths of a nation are buried along with the bodies. Illegally disappeared and sacrilegiously buried (without the proper rituals by the families) these sites literally are on the map of the land and not on it. But these sites mean something more.

Yet sites of the dead remain linked to the living. Diana Kontsevaia speaking of the mass graves in Srebrenica writes:

> dead bodies occupy a specific physical space, claiming the territory for the group of people who are related to the deceased … Despite attempts to deemphasize territory, it continues to play an important role in the politics of the living, especially in the reburial of past victims. As a result, the territory a memorial occupies is significant because it re-organizes the territorial boundaries of an ethnic group. (2013: 17–18)

There are two parts to this theme of burial and reburial in HR texts.

First, landscapes of disappearances such as the ones in *Of Love and Shadows*, *Naming the Spirits* and *Anil's Ghost* are not marked as *graves*. They are secret graves, so to speak, in which the country's secrets are buried along with the bodies. I adapt this image of the burial of a country's secrets from Lawrence Thornton's *Naming the Spirits*:

> The members of the unit spoke only when necessary, conscious of being watched, isolated by their work that was binding everyone together as they *dug into the country's sorrow and its shame*. (238, emphasis added)

These are places used for the interment of the disappeared. Living people have disappeared, and not even their bodies remain. Families and communities have nothing to mourn over—since the regime disappears the living and the dead.

The absence of a body, a proper burial site or memorial ensures that the families cannot ever mourn their disappeared. This also means that the landscape of disappearances is one where the families are never certain that their disappeared are *dead*, simply because the bodies are also disappeared. This is a zone of indistinction *par excellence* because not only is the line between disappeared-but-alive and disappeared-and-dead left uncertain and blurred, but also because the line between living *body* and dead *body* is no longer drawable since there is no body at all. What disappears, then, is the very possibility of accounting for the living or the dead.

Second, the mass graves are zones of indistinction in another crucial way: the borders of individuals and families can no longer be ascertained because the bones and remains are all merged, mixed up. In *Naming the Spirits*, the spirit of one of the disappeared, says: 'by the next afternoon they had recovered all of us' (245).

> Then the sorting began, the search for clues. Our still-mute bones were marked with pieces of tape and numbered. Matted, blood-stained clothes were laid out in rows through which Roberto strayed like a derelict, staring at the array of shirts, dresses, shoes, jewelry, his hope bolstered by the fact that the earring had not been his daughter's. (245–246)

The diggers sort through 'Adidas athletic shoes, men's. Woman's shoe with stiletto heel, no mate. Three silver bracelets with markings …' (246). The spirit comments: 'That's all we were to the spectators, a neat array of femurs, tibias, skulls, metacarpals attended by what remained of the things we'd worn' (247). In *Of Love and Shadows* the investigators unearth bones, skulls, a 'trunk with shreds of clothing; shirts and socks of various colours; a pelvic bone; and various additional bones' (235). Nobody knows whose bodies these are, admits Faustino Rivera (249). In *Murambi*, some bodies, says Siméon to Cornelius, 'are intact'. He adds: 'during the first days, you could recognize certain people. Some of the Murambi townspeople know which ones are their relatives among the remains' ('Murambi'). Stories about the disappeared alone remain, suggesting that the disappeared are at once alive and interred in the narratives. Minoli Salgado puts it this way: 'the real story falls into a narrative vacuum where bodies disappear, and thus keeping open a space for the possibility of redemption and return' (215). In *Anil's Ghost, Naming the Spirits, Of Love and Shadows, In the Shadow of the Banyan*, therefore, people speak of the ones they have lost, and never found.

For the surviving relations of the disappeared the mass grave is no grave at all because the bodies of their immediate family members are indistinguishable in this mass of bones and belongings. Thus mass graves become part of a landscape of disappearance by virtue of interring those individuals who have disappeared, who are now dead, but in the process rendering the dead indistinguishable from each other. In effect, dead family members also *disappear* into the mass of dead bodies. Thus Doctor Karekazi 'gave orders to make [the thousands of bodies] disappear' ('Colonel Étienne Perrin') as a mode of not just disappearing people but disappearing their traces and their social identities as well.

The disappeared are unavailable for legal, humanitarian and historical purposes of the community (I follow here the work of Kirsten Juhl and Odd Einar Olsen, 2006, in investigating mass graves). They cannot be 'claimed' as evidence for prosecuting those responsible for the disappearances, and thus are also at the heart of a disappearance of the very possibility of legal processes. They are unavailable for families and communities to achieve closure for their dead since there are no clearly identifiable bodies, and sometimes no bodies at all—indicating a disappearance of humanitarian possibilities. 'Blacks feel strongly about the bones of their relatives', says the farmer to Sarah Barcant in *Red Dust*, 'they never leave them unclaimed' (261).

Finally, with unidentifiable bodies, there is no possibility of a historical record. Mass graves therefore constitute a series of disappearances all of which have to do with the community's identity as much as with the individual, grieving family's.

Dumped in anonymous, even unknown, places such as the mines in *Of Love and Shadows*, the sea in *Anil's Ghost*, the grove in *Naming the Spirits*, the desert in *Sandcastle Girls*, an unidentified place in *The Truth Commissioner* and the forests in *The Persistence of Memory*, the dead may no longer be appropriated by the community for its own purposes of identity and identification. There is only an undifferentiated mass of bones, notes Armen in *Sandcastle Girls*: 'he can't imagine how many bodies it took to make the hillock. Hundreds? A thousand? More?' (123) At the camp in Der-el-Zor, Elizabeth looks out and 'squints at the rows of the dead and dying'. 'The bodies', she registers, 'stretch all the way to the small hill' (152). There appears little to distinguish the living from the dead in that scene, a point echoed by Jessica in *Murambi* when she hears that the French army has finally arrived to end the massacre of the Tutsis: 'We'll see how they manage to save the lives of people who've been dead for such a long time' ('Jessica'). Cornelius viewing the remains in the Murambi Polytechnic School notes:

> The bodies, which were covered with a fine layer of mud, were almost all intact. Without his being able to say why, the remains in Murambi gave him the impression of still being alive. ('Murambi')

Since the living are always linked to *their* dead, as Kontsevaia notes, mass and unidentified graves represent the end of one mode of the *living's* self-fashioning—via their dead—although, paradoxically, in all HR texts, the living also fashion themselves as mourners for their lost ones. Once again reinforcing the idea of a zone of indistinction, mass and unmarked graves represent the blurring of lines between individual identity and communitarian identity through an appropriation of their dead.

Zones of indistinction, especially those between life and death, the living and the dead, are also created due to a return of nature to reclaim the dead: returning the body to nature, as it were. For example, when Cornelius is viewing the remains in the school, Gerard who accompanies him informs him that 'the bodies are intact because there's clay in the soil there' ('Murambi'). The bodies are thus located at the intersection of the living and the non-living, but organic all the same. In *Sandcastle Girls*, Elizabeth wonders why some skulls have grass growing through them, until a gendarme points out that it was not grass, but hair: 'the skulls were spouting great black tresses of hair' (154). The ruined body is interred in the landscape for nature to work its processes: eventually the body will be reclaimed by natural processes of growth of vegetation or decay. With this the distinction between the landscape and the human body is blurred.

Ghostification and Uncanny Revelation

'She [his mother] ended up being killed ... And her body is here. Lost among thousands of others,' says Cornelius in *Murambi* viewing the pile of unidentifiable bones and skulls at the site of the greatest massacre during the Rwandan genocide ('Murambi'). The inability to isolate his mother from the rest agonizes him, and compounds the tragedy of survivors in *Murambi*. In Czeslaw Milosz's 'Child of Europe' he writes towards the end:

> He who invokes history is always secure.
> The dead will not rise to witness against him.
>
> You can accuse them of any deeds you like.
> Their reply will always be silence.
>
> Their empty faces swim out of the deep dark.
> You can fill them with any features desired.
>
> (in Forché 442)

The dead become 'everyman' and 'everywoman' in Milosz's poem, and in the process signify not only the indignity of anonymity but also the oppressive categorization into whatever the regime wants them to be. They are ghosts whose origins in specific human lives, contexts and processes are erased so that they can be ghosts of what the state wants to deploy.

A bag of bones, writes Avery Gordon, 'only aims to eradicate "any meaning that death might have in society"' (115). Disappearance is 'a state-sponsored procedure for producing ghosts to harrowingly haunt a population into submission' (115). Disappearance 'involves controlling the imagination, controlling the meaning of death, involves creating new identities' (124). The disappeared lose 'all social and political identity: no bureaucratic records, no funerals, no memorials, no bodies, nobody' (80). The 'epistemological doubt [around disappearance] is itself a form of domination' (80).

Epistemological doubt and secrecy are weapons of mass destruction, where the subject populations are terrified into submission under threat of being anonymized, or having their loved ones anonymized. The state's rhetoric, exemplified in the General's instructions in *Of Love and Shadows*, the official instructions at the end of *Anil's Ghost*, the Khmer speeches in *In the Shadow of the Banyan*, generates not information but secrecy and illusion (of progress, of equality). But the HR text's response to the official construction of doubt, secrecy and illusion is to 'produce' ghosts and anonymized bodies as counterevidence, offering a limited knowledge of the actions of the government. Thus, the land reveals bodies in an uncanny uncovering of what should have remained hidden.[1] All these texts, therefore, oscillate between the themes of *ghostification*—people rendered into ghosts either by pushing them into the zone of indistinction where they live close to death or by literally exterminating them—and *uncanny revelation* of buried secrets.

In *Sandcastle Girls* the Armenians are deprived of their passports and then sent out into the desert camps to be tortured or starved to death. Consequently, there are no clues as to the identities of the dead. In *Anil's Ghost* three key disappearances—Sailor, Sirissa, Sarath—are described without description, so to speak. Sailor is of course the skeleton that Anil and Sarath are trying to identify. We assume that Anil gets out of Sri Lanka, but the novel does not explicitly state this. Sarath becomes one of the disappeared but not anonymized because his body arrives on his doctor brother, Gamini's table (287–290). The vehicles that picked up the school students and staff, Sarath tells Anil, 'had no number plates' (185), and thus remained anonymous and untraceable. The dead are consigned to anonymity, and worse, to the realm of the 'suicides'. Unclaimed bodies occur frequently in *Anil's Ghost* (176, 184–185, 212–213), as also in *In the Shadow of the Banyan* (305). Ratner references ghosts too (306). In *Naming the Spirits* and *Of Love and Shadows* the community seeks to identify their dead buried in mass graves. Skeletons and signs of hasty burials dot the landscape outside Aleppo in *Sandcastle Girls*. 'You'll never learn any more of what happened to her [Karine],' Elizabeth says to Armen about his wife (64).

Despite the ghostification efforts of the state, HR texts suggest in their spectropoetics, there is an inevitable collapse of secret processes: skeletons are (literally) revealed. In several cases this uncanny revelation is literally an uncovering of bodies: in *Sandcastle Girls*, *Murambi*, *Of Love and Shadows*, *Naming the Spirits*, and other texts, where bodies have been doubly anonymized by first having all identification erased and then buried in places that do not exist on maps. In *Naming the Spirits*, it is the sole survivor of a massacre, who leads the people to the secret mass graves, but the story itself is narrated by the spirits of the killed. In *Anil's Ghost* the skeleton, Anil and Sarath hope, will reveal the state's oppressive history: 'the skeleton I had was evidence of a certain kind of crime,' says Anil (275).

If ghostification is the state's process of anonymizing citizens, the uncanny revelations of bodies and people, suggests the HR text, is the unveiling of *embodied* state secrets. Johannes Bobrowski describes such a nightmarish embodiment of a nation's history in 'Pruzzian Elegy':

> Then in the forests of the homeland
> ---
> We shuddered
> Where groves had smoked
> With sacrifice, before stones,
> By long sunken-in gravemounds,
>
> (in Forché 445)

Bobrowski is speaking at the transformation of groves into graves, a transformation that literally embodies the change in the nation itself as manifest in the anonymized bodies buried there. The bodies, the 'people/ of smouldering groves', as Bobrowski puts it towards the end of the poem (Forché 446), embody the lies of the state, and offer up knowledge that defeats the attempts at ghostification. Now the phantom, Nicholas Rand reminds us, has 'the potential to illuminate the genesis of social institutions' (169). Ghosts are signs of institutional processes, and bodies are uncanny material evidence—because they reveal what should not be revealed—of the ghostification and anonymization of people by the state. Wasted bodies of the nearly-dead are also embodied evidence. *Sandcastle Girls* in its opening pages describes the Armenian women ('deportees', as they are termed by the Turkish authorities in the novel) being marched through the town, and the American, Elizabeth, is watching them, appalled. The women are 'beyond modesty, beyond caring ... their skin has been seared black by the sun or stained by the soil in which they have slept or, in some cases, by great yawning scabs and wounds' (13). To Elizabeth they look like 'dying wild animals' (13) and she thinks of them as 'skeletons' (13) and on another occasion as 'catatonic skeletons in rags' (47). After months of abuse the comfort women in *A Gesture Life* are reduced to 'skeletons' (302), although not quite dead. When forced to relocate from their palace, Raami, sitting in a truck with her family, sees herself as reduced to a 'skeleton of [her] former sel[f]' (*In the Shadow of the Banyan*, 150). In some cases she assumes the women are old, even grandmothers, until a fellow American at the Embassy tells her the women look old because 'severe malnourishment will do that to you' (30). They too occupy the zone of indistinction. The dying and the living, the dead and the nearly-dead among the tortured and the deported in these texts are evidentiary bodies. Even dematerialized bodies, such as the ones Francisco and Irene unearth in *Of Love and Shadows*, offer evidence and unpack secret knowledge about the state.[2] This could very well be, suggests the Romanian poet Ion Caraion in 'Remember', an 'anti-history' (in Forché 453). Caraion writes of 'railway stations swathed in ghosts' and immediately recalls the *history* of Jews being transported across Europe towards the concentration and extermination camps. It serves as an anti-history because it refutes official histories of the state preferring, instead, to focus on the ghosts who bring back a particular past.

Bishnupriya Ghosh, in her reading of Amitav Ghosh's 1997 novel *The Calcutta Chromosome* (1997), argues that ghosts in Amitav Ghosh's fiction occupy a 'redemptive place' and force us to ask certain 'questions of political justice and hope' (2004: 205). Spectres, she writes, 'collapse the boundaries of present, past and future' (206). They are redemptive because they are witnesses to the erasure of certain people in the present. Certain people simply do not count in the imagining of communities and nations (207–208). Emerging out of the earth as phantoms, spirits (*Naming the Spirits*) or plain dead bodies (*Of Love and Shadows, Murambi, Anil's Ghost*), or existing in the border zone of death and life (in *Sandcastle Girls*, in particular but also the march of the injured dispossessed in *The Farming of Bones*), these groups of people and communities in HR texts serve as commentaries on the state's politics. Dispossessed of homes, identities and bodies, they are ghosts. They cannot lead a 'normal' existence anywhere: the Haitians in *The Farming of Bones*, for instance, are forced to march to safety; Raami's family evicted from their palace in *In the Shadow of the Banyan* is relocated to a distant village, the Tutsis are chased from their lands and homesteads and then killed in *Murambi*. The history of these places, in other words, is a history of both ghostification and uncanny revelations.

By uncanny revelations I also wish to signal the return of repressed memories. Mass graves, suggests Jennifer Sime, 'reveal the present as itself a scene of absence where the return of memory dislocates the present from itself' (2013: 10). Sime elaborates:

> They [skulls and bones in mass graves] are horrific in part because of their anonymity; because these skulls are, at once, absolutely unique (we know this skull belongs to someone, but to whom?) and because these skulls index the multitude of other anonymous bodies that lie in mass graves—those for whom the processes of exhumation, identification, and individuation will never arrive. The anonymity allows us to participate in an uncanny moment of recognition for, as Maurice Blanchot has noted, the cadaver presences a dislocation that ordinarily remains hidden; that is, the pull from the singular toward the generic and neutral that shadows every body. (Blanchot 1982: 258) (Sime 49)

In keeping with the uncanny, then, the skeletons and bones exhumed by Irene and Francisco in *Of Love and Shadows* or the heap of skeletons that Armene and then Elizabeth in *Sandcastle Girls* see in the desert outside Aleppo are at once familiar and strange: they are human but not an *identifiable* individual human. In a sense the uncanny revelation reinforces the ghostification for many survivors precisely because there is no way of ascertaining the identity of their loved and dead ones. They remain familiar as humans but distant as individuals. Uncanny revelations are far more troubling than the sense of loss, as Cornelius discovers in *Murambi*:

> But why did these rooms piled with corpses make him think of life rather than of death? Perhaps of the way their arms were stretched out toward the Interahamwe in a last absurd plea? A forest of arms still murmuring with the cries of terror and despair. ('Murambi')

The man showing him around tells him: 'You'll see the same bodies everywhere'. And Cornelius thinks: 'Each one of these corpses had had a life that was different from that of all the others' ('Murambi'). When swimming in the Massacre River (bordering Haiti and the Dominican Republic), Amabelle says, 'every now and then … a swimmer finds a set of white spongy bones, a skeleton, thinned by time and being buried too long in the riverbed' (Danticat 307–308).

The dead—revealed, exposed and exhumed—reappear in the lives of survivors. They are the past returned into the present, defining it in some way. They are at once familiar and strange. Steve's remains, for example, when exhumed in *Red Dust*, appear in the form of a 'completely disintegrated body, a long, thin, angular, unwieldy shape' (264). Two bags, containing a watch and a pair of sneakers, are also exhumed (264). It is at the sight of the latter that Mrs Sizela, Steve's mother, begins wailing (264). Unspeakably horrible deaths, such as Steve's, Sarath's (*Anil's Ghost*) or Connor Walshe's (*The Truth Commissioner*) leave behind remnants that serve as instruments of both memorialization (Steve's shoes, the tape Sarath leaves behind for Anil, the tape with Connor Walshe's voice, the book of poems Raami's father leaves for her, the scraps of paper from Susana in *Requiem for a Woman's Soul*, among other examples) and revivification. In *Naming the Spirits*, the book Cecilia writes about her experiences in prison (the subject of the earlier novel, *Imagining Argentina*), is, in her own view, 'like a skeleton, with missing bones' (65). These are instruments that integrate the past into the present, often functioning (except in the case of Cecilia's book, since she does not die in the novels), as *material* traces of the ghost, of the disappeared.

Mass graves are modes of uncanny revelation in another sense. James Tyner elaborates:

> The mass grave indicates, further, assemblages and administrative structures that produce death on a large scale. Mass graves can no longer be viewed only (or predominantly) as visible reminders of past violence; rather mass graves appear as key indicators into the administrative governance of a society. (2014: 72)

In a comment that illustrates Tyner's insistence on the link between past violence, present-day mourning and administrative governance Lawrence Thornton in *Naming the Spirits* writes:

> [Roberto] had become aware that he was exactly like thousands of others deprived of the story that could fill the space hollowed out below their

> hearts by the generals. Because not knowing was torture. No one could grieve properly, wring their hearts out when the last pages were missing. It was as if time had stopped for all of them. (181)

Thornton is describing an entire society unable to grieve.

In an earlier chapter I discussed the socio-institutional structures that are eroded and thus produce torture and death. I now propose that this 'erosion' consists of the strengthening of particular aspects of administrative processes. For instance, in *Sandcastle Girls*, the Turkish administration systematically collects passports and identification papers from the Armenians (91–92, 142). Special cells and structures are set up in the prison and penal system to enable the construction of torture cells and mass graves. In *The Truth Commissioner* we are told that the police employed young boys as informants. James Fenton admits at the TRC: 'In the fight against terrorism it was of crucial importance to gather intelligence. We needed that intelligence to try to protect life' (331). Fenton admits, in short, that structures and administrative processes were put in place to investigate terror but, as the novel reveals, also enabled the exploitation and eventual killing of a boy-informant. What the skeletal remains reveal, in addition to the fact of death, is that some processes enabled the regimes to send these people to their death. Mass graves therefore place on display the power of the state to expose thousands of people to death.

Even when the believed-to-be-dead return, as happens with Teresa (believed dead in *Imagining Argentina*) in *Naming the Spirits*, they are very often ghostly. Thornton writes in the latter book of Teresa's return to Carlos and Cecilia:

> Carlos knew her place in the family was destined to be as bright and ghostly as a hologram. Light and shadow, flesh and spirit, she had ridden his half-told story back into the world. (253)

Heterotopias

In *Sandcastle Girls*, the women and girls are taken away to 'resettlement camps', described as 'desert wastelands without food or shelter or, sometimes, even water' (54). These are places of death, not resettlement. In *Anil's Ghost* the bodies that wash up on the beach are known, publicly, as 'victims of torture in the house on Gower Street or a house off the Galle Road' (212). Sarath informs Anil that 'there are two unauthorized places of detention in Colombo. One of the locations is off Havelock Road in Kollupitiya' (135). It is almost as though the hidden and unauthorized place is barely hidden. They are identifiable locations in the city's geography. In other cases, such as *The Truth Commissioner, Red Dust, Imagining Argentina*, the arrested and disappeared are taken to abandoned warehouses and farmhouses to be tortured—the location of these spaces are not often known.

The unidentified bodies are, despite the erasure of identification, political bodies. The disappeared too, like unidentified bodies, are political bodies. Together, the unidentified and the disappeared constitute a paradox: they are at once secret and public (Perera 2006: 650). In the first case they conceal a secret that is public: this was a tortured and murdered individual, but whose identity, like the identity of the torturer and/or killer may never be known. In the second case, families and communities know that some of them have been disappeared—the disappearance is common knowledge—but the current location, or status (alive? dead?) may never be known. These are places where the secret and the hidden become visible, but also reveal the processes that enabled the bodies to be *produced* in particular ways by eroding their autonomy, dignity and integrity.

Places of torture, such as the Naval Mechanics School (*The Little School, Imagining Argentina*) or 'house on Gower Street or a house off the Galle Road' (*Anil's Ghost*), the 'clandestine prison' (*Imagining Argentina* 47), are spaces where the relations between the state and its citizens are inverted, even destroyed. Peter Johnson's interpretation of Foucauldian heterotopias defines them as 'sites which are embedded in aspects and stages of our lives and which somehow mirror and at the same time distort, unsettle or invert other spaces' (2013: 790). The heterotopia 'disturbs and unsettles wherever it sheds its light: cultural spaces, disciplinary borders and notions of subjectivity' (800). It is a *dispositif*, 'both an abstract machine and a concrete assemblage' (800). And further: 'heterotopian sites do not sit in isolation as reservoirs of freedom, emancipation or resistance; they coexist, combine and connect. They are not stable entities; they are contingent qualities' (800). One needs to see heterotopias as 'both an empirical *and* conceptual starting point for analysis' (800, emphasis in original).

Heterotopias in HR texts are *places* where a set of *practices* may be carried out with impunity, in order to invert relations and unsettle the subjectivities of both victim and perpetrator. They are assemblages of place, practice and people. Therefore we can treat specific places as heterotopic but also see heterotopias as emerging through particular kinds of practices, such as torture or inflicted suffering.

Places like the Naval Mechanics School, the prison in Smits river (*Red Dust*) are woven into the very fabric of everyday lives, but something out of the ordinary social and juridical relations occurs in them. The state tests its powers of sovereignty by eroding the psychological and corporeal integrity of individuals in HR texts. Constructed as places of legal procedures, these spaces function as heterotopias due to their deployment of extra-legal procedures like torture.

Heterotopias are places where citizen-subjects are reassigned values: as subversives, threats, dissidents or terrorists. This enables the state apparatus to inflict grievous harm upon them, further eroding their identity as citizen-subjects.

In *A Gesture Life*, the comfort women are described as 'female volunteers' (160) and housed inside the military camp. The process of acquiring these volunteers, Hata as senior officer assures his subordinate, is routine: 'to assure the corporal of the commonness of all our procedures' (162). Yet, he thinks to himself: 'the imminent arrival of these "volunteers," as they were referred to, seemed quite removed from the ordinary' (162). Now the camp is converted into a heterotopic space through a process of degraded Othering inflicted upon the Korean women, having first denied them all human dignity. The ordinary camp is rendered extraordinary through this process. Nothing about it is quite common, as Hata recognizes but refuses to admit to the corporal.

The resettlement camp in *Sandcastle Girls* is a heterotopia where Armenians might be exposed to death under the pretence of relocation and safety. First, as Ryan informs Elizabeth about the camps: 'the Turks have built the sort of pens you might see on a cattle ranch' (144). Bodies are 'allowed to bleed out as if they were wild game. Deer.Turkey, Moose' (144). Second, the Armenians are not always killed immediately, but they are reduced, through constant exposure to death from the cold, starvation and thirst, to inhuman states. Rather than 'consolidating' the Armenians in one place by securing them, as the official discourse claims (90), the camp becomes an inhuman heterotopic extension of the march into the desert. The Turks execute the Armenian women, picked randomly from the convoy marching into the desert, by tying them to stakes and charging them on horses and decapitating them. The whole process, recalls a survivor, Nevart, looked like 'a mere cavalry exercise' (66).

In other HR texts everyday spaces are rendered heterotopic. For a brief period of time Lydia's home in *Bitter Fruit* becomes heterotopic when DuBoise rapes her in it. As a display of racialized sovereignty, and empowered by apparatuses of power (he is a policeman), DuBoise's actions destroy not only Lydia's corporeal integrity and subjectivity but also the integrity and subjectivity of her home and the cultural space of her marriage: her husband is shackled inside a police van outside their home so that he can hear her screams. In *Disgrace*, similarly, Lucy is raped within her home with her father injured and locked up in an adjacent room, again an act that inverts the sovereignty of their home. In such cases and spaces, Peter Johnson notes citing De Cauter and Deheane, 'appearance is hidden, but where the hidden appears' (798). What is hidden are the social and institutional structures that enable acts like rape and violation, but it is also possible to make these structures manifest within those acts of violence against bodies and people.

These are spaces where camaraderie and friendship, trust and faith are eroded so that husbands and wives betray each other, just as friends and comrades do. Undermining the foundation of social relations, heterotopian spaces instil, instead, fear, guilt and shame as the foundations of a new social order. In Sarath's words in *Anil's Ghost*, 'I wanted to find one law to cover all of living. I found fear' (135). In all HR texts, social relations are re-established on the foundations of this one law: fear.

Seeing these spaces as heterotopic for their role in inverting social relations is, however, only one way of examining the prison, the camp and the farmhouse in HR texts.

HR texts posit crypts as locations, architectural and cultural-psychological, for not just individuals but also for entire communities. They are effects of failed or incomplete mourning and represent the silencing of violent histories which then erupts in the form of phantoms.

Communities and Mourning

'Carlos would find a way to place his grief among the griefs of the city's people,' writes Lawrence Thornton in *Imagining Argentina* (31). In HR texts mass graves, deaths and disappearances mobilize a community through a culture of mourning, but also the impossibility of mourning. While they steer away from speaking of memorials or formal rituals of mourning, the texts are suffused with a *discourse* of mourning and memorialization.

This culture of mourning in HR texts is linked in many cases to language and narrative.

The Mobilization of Mourning

'A happy nation has no memory. That's the problem with this country, we want to forgive but we don't want to forget. You can't have it both ways.' This is Alec's thought in *Bitter Fruit* (86). It captures a key theme in HR texts: the mobilization of not only memory but of mourning as a defining feature of societies that have seen genocides and totalitarianism.

Communities in HR texts are built around memories of terror and mourning. But they are also mobilized, especially in texts centred around TRCs and institutionalized recall, in a process of 'healing' and reconciliation. Memory and mourning, therefore, are not only defining features of the afflicted community, they are also states the community must go beyond in order to heal.

In *Imagining Argentina* the prosecutor has finished his summation of the crimes the generals had perpetrated. The process of prosecution is described through the eyes of the narrator Martin Benn, the journalist. The passage describes a community brought together in shared suffering, memory and the possibility of mourning through the narrative of the prosecution and the witness accounts. Benn reports:

> For seventeen numbing weeks we had listened to the charges and seen the horrible proofs—photographs and bones, an old woman pointing a shaking finger, a teenaged boy making his way to the witness stand on crutches. *Everyone* who attended the trial understood what had been done, and the wounds *we all bore* were opened each time a witness spoke. Yet what had happened to our friends and families could not be fitted into the statistics, for the numbers were impossible to believe, and toward the end the charges began to take on the abstraction of a mathematical formula …
>
> The people listened attentively, quietly, and they might have been civilized people anywhere until I saw their eyes filling with the blood and terror of memory, the handiwork of these graying men in the dock before me. (211–212, emphasis added)

In *Of Love and Shadows* families of the disappeared begin to appear in the town square carrying photographs—what I termed 'melancholy objects' in Chap. 3—of their missing ones. In *The Truth Commissioner* David Park writes:

> The families of the victims have started to reclaim their dead and forgotten loved ones and given this brief moment of public restoration, they parade to the chamber [of the TRC] carrying portraits of their murdered relatives and candles ... The portraits of the children are the most disturbing as they force the viewer to try and project how they now would look. (246)

In his pedantic and rather pompous speech, the 'truth commissioner', Henry Stanfield, states:

> We meet to give a voice to the victims of the violence, to remember those who have died or suffered and try to help those who grieve to take the difficult and painful step toward healing. Without this individual healing there can be no societal healing and without confronting our past in a spirit of reconciliation and understanding society can never build a better future ... Truth is vital if this society is to open itself to the possibility of communal atonement. (317)

In *Red Dust* Alex Mpondo, looking around the TRC hall thinks:

> What they had in common was not just their shared suffering but the manner in which they had all been forced to keep their humanity by generalising it. To each of them in different ways the collective had become more important than the individual—not just because this made political sense but because it was one way of surviving all that pain. (171)

Mpondo also recalls the slogan at funerals: 'don't mourn, mobilise' (171). Trying to recall his friend Steve, Mpondo 'ended up ... scrolling through frozen portraits of the other dead' and realizes that it was 'so hard to mourn them all' (170–171).

In each of these cases we see a mobilization of individual mourning into collective mourning. Institutionalized processes of recall such as the TRCs or trials become, in HR texts, cultural spaces where individuals and families find themselves bound together into a community of suffering. HR texts posit an oscillation between individual and collective mourning, often proposing, as we can see in the passages above, the tension between the two. The institutional recall directed at 'healing' revisits and opens up old wounds, as studies have shown (Dawes 2007; Payne 2008). The process of documenting disappearances and death become in these texts processes of mobilizing individual mourning into a larger ***discursive memorial*** for and of the community itself. Writing about mass graves and memorials in Srebernica, C.E. Pollack argues that families who were politically isolated preferred to have burial sites so they could simply mourn their loved ones, while politically active families/individuals wanted burial sites to serve political ends (2003).

Personal memories, such as the ones each of these texts details, are 'embodied memories' that contribute to a nation's collective memory. Marita Sturken writes of this process of merging the two:

> When personal memories are deployed in the context of marking the anniversary of historical events, they are presented either as the embodied evidence of history or as evidence of history's failures. Survivors return to the sites of their war experience; they place their bodies within the discourse of remembering either to affirm history's narratives or to declare them incomplete, incapable of conjuring their experience. They represent a very particular form of embodied memory. While history functions much more smoothly in the absence of survivors, and survivors are often dissenting voices to history's narratives, history making also accords to them a very particular authority as the embodiment of authentic experience. (1997: 688)

The individual's memories in HR texts become a subset of the national narrative with its sub-narratives of atonement, forgiveness, justice, truth and reconciliation. Each of these sub-narratives serves as a 'national symbolic' (Berlant cited in Sturken 688). But the HR texts, as we can see from the emphasis on terror (Thornton) or 'generalized' humanity that ignores the individual (*Red Dust*), calls into question such a national symbolic by proposing, as Alec insinuates in *Bitter Fruit*, the primacy of mourning over any other public feeling. The inconsolable mourning is the foundation of a discursive memorial which, in the absence of a more bricks-and-mortar memorial, serves as a reminder and remainder of a troubled past. More than the national symbolic of reconciliation or atonement—the ostensible generative myth of processes like the TRCs—it is the *national symbolic of mourning* that HR texts foreground. Memory does not effect reconciliation in the community: it mobilizes sadness so that the national symbolic remains marked, for all practical purposes, by inconsolable mourning.

Language and Mourning

The nameless girl-survivor of Thornton's *Naming the Spirits* starts speaking volubly about disappeared people. Mercedes listens to her and then reports to her husband, Roberto, of 'the way each [narrative] ended as if clipped off in mid-sentence, suggestive of a loose connection, a short-circuit, or perhaps merely a sudden lack of words or the will to speak them' (231–232). It becomes difficult, as Gabriela and Mercedes discover, to unravel the girl's narrative which seems to gesture at something horrific and significant, but intangible.

HR texts have numerous such references to fragmentations, distortions, gaps and ellipses in the language of trauma victims, what psychoanalysts have called 'cryptonymy' (Abraham and Török 1986). Elaborating this idea, Gabriele Schwab discusses the crypt as a 'burial place inside the self for a love object that is lost but kept inside the self as a living corpse' (Schwab 2010: 45). The crypt contains 'secrets and silences formed in trauma' (45). Looking at an exhumed skeleton 'was like reading a diary someone had left open on a table', writes Thornton in *Naming the* Spirits (180–181). The forensic experts tell Roberto in the same novel: 'they [the disinterred bones] all have stories to tell, but they're slow to speak' (183). In works like *Anil's Ghost*, *Of Love and Shadows* and *Naming the Spirits* the language to be decoded is the language of bones, disinterred from the mass, unmarked graves so that their families would have a body to grieve over. Coetzee's Magistrate seeks to 'read' the ruins and the wooden 'slips' with engraved characters he finds in the vicinity of his camp. In Horst Bienek's 'Our Ashes', the ghost of a dead man/woman describes being killed and 'quick-lime delet[ing] our faces' (lime was used to destroy the bones of the dead during the Holocaust) and then concludes the poem with the evidentiary value of *any* remnants:

> We have chlorine in the eyes
> And sand in the ears
> And eternity
>   grows silently in our bodies
>
> When will our ashes speak?
>
> (in Forché 473)

Yet, the language of skeletons and skulls is about more than just grieving families: as they are disinterred and decoded they reveal the presence of a cultural crypt that ensured, for a very long time, incomplete mourning for a whole community.

HR texts posit the crypt at both the individual-psychological and communitarian-cultural levels for, as Schwab proposes, there can be 'collective crypts, communal crypts, and even national crypts' (46). In the first instance, HR texts offer examples of encrypted language with distortions and silences that require decoding. Noting a parallel between *Waiting for the Barbarians* and *Anil's Ghost*, James Dawes writes:

> Both feature, as one of their key subplots, the attempt by a main character to translate an ancient language recently rediscovered—and both, interestingly, involve a critical moment when the translator insists to authorities that the language can be read when, in fact, it can't. These acts of translation find their thematic echo in the continual return within these texts to acts of translating across other barriers. In *Anil's Ghost:* translating the symbols readable in damaged bodies and unburied skeletons, translating bodily signals to situate oneself in a strange and hostile environment, translating the non sequiturs of a friend suffering from dementia, translating difficult texts ... In *Waiting for the Barbarians:* translating or failing to translate the meaning of scars in a tortured body, translating or failing to translate overheard speech and sounds, and translating or failing to translate across the language border with the barbarians. (Dawes 2007: 218–219)

Lakma in *Anil's Ghost* witnesses her parents' violent death and lapses into an interminable silence. Ondaatje writes: 'Lakma watched him [her uncle Palipana] and listened, never speaking, a silent amanuensis for his whispered histories' (172). As Victoria Burrows presciently points out, listening is central to the novel (2008: 174–175). I take 'listening' as a trope for 'reading' but also for decoding, recognition and acknowledgment of a not-too-clear, or visible, trauma. Thus Sarath, as Anil discovers, 'was always whispering. She [Anil] kept saying, *What? What?* [but after a while] [c]ould hardly bother to say it' (60). It is only later in the novel that Sarath speaks to her of the 'law' of fear that governs all living so that we, like Anil, make the connection between fear and the whisper, the fear of articulation and enunciation. He warns Anil: 'it's sometimes more dangerous here to *tell* the truth' (53, emphasis added). Sarath makes sure that Anil's tape recorder is off before he speaks of the culture of fear (135). At the end of the novel, giving her the opportunity to expose the truth about the culture of fear and the executions, Sarath records his final message to Anil. Ondaatje writes:

> His [Sarath's] voice came on, very clear and focused. He must have held the recorder close to his mouth as he whispered … She walked away from the skeleton and paced up and down listening to his voice again. Listening to everything again. (284)

During the long march in *Sandcastle Girls*, Hatoun 'never complained, but only because she had stopped speaking' (67). She is described as a 'scarred and silent child' after having witnessed her mother's execution (268). In *Waiting for the Barbarians*, the Magistrate tries very hard to make the tortured, blind girl to speak about whatever had been done to her. Lucy and Lydia refuse to speak about their rape in *Disgrace* and *Bitter Fruit*. Gabriela in *Naming the Spirits* pays close attention to the words the nameless girl-survivor uses. The spirits try to aid Gabriela in her efforts to unravel the events the girl has witnessed:

> We encouraged her to use her abilities to ferret out connections so she could map a semblance of the world from the girl's enthusiastic but broken speech. But … Gabriela could not find the key. Her ability to tease the deepest meanings from her texts … proved useless in deciphering what she heard. (161)

One of the most intriguing modes of gesturing at the crypt born of trauma occurs in Loh's *Breaking the Tongue*. Claude briefly narrates his tortures and his earwitness to Ling-Li's in the adjacent cell. But the key passages where he details the last moments of Ling-Li are in Chinese. The Chinese passages in the novel are left untranslated. Now, Claude has never learnt his mother tongue, having been brought up in an Anglophile family. That he chooses to practise his mother tongue at the testamentary moment and in a testimonial narrative suggests an encryption of the trauma within Claude's language. (The title of the novel itself seems to indicate a cryptonymy.) The sequence of narration, alternating between Chinese and an occasional English word or two, writes Stephanie Althey, 'both depicts and obscures the scene of torture' (2012: 192). The shift from his primary language, English, to Chinese to bear witness—as Ling-Li, appearing in Claude's dreams, had instructed him to (480–481)—might be read as the fragmentation, even dissolution, of Claude's language as much as a return to his mother tongue in the face of trauma. However, there is more to this 'linguistic blockade' (as Julia Lovell termed it in her review of the novel, 2006) than either encryption or linguistic shift. Like the silence of the torture victim and/or witness in *Sandcastle Girls*, *Disgrace* or *Bitter Fruit*, we need to listen to the Chinese rendering of witness accounts as a mode of both articulating *and* masking silenced histories—of Armenians (*Sandcastle Girls*), Sarajevans (*The Cellist of Sarajevo*), white women (*Disgrace*), black women (*Bitter Fruit*, *Waiting for the Barbarians*), and Chinese (*Breaking the Tongue*). That is, I see encryption through the modes of silencing and linguistic shift as a cultural encryption of an entire community's torture and subsequent silencing. The silencing of trauma, Schwab constantly reminds us, results in their appearance in stories (2010). In the fragmented, aleatory and often strange language we discern the crypt into which the tortured individuals and communities consign their memories. Thus we need to see the silences as larger than mental no-go crypts but rather as the cultural crypt wherein the entire community's silencing has confined its memories.

The tortured body is metonymic of the cultural crypt and a community's silencing, the collapse of a language for its trauma. Thus, the reason for Hatoun's silence, we realize, is that she has been traumatized by what she has seen in the desert (*Sandcastle Girls*). The blind 'barbarian' girl in *Waiting for the Barbarians*, likewise, is unable to speak after her torture and Claude in *Breaking the Tongue* has nightmares where he cuts out his tongue. Given the fact that they have been tortured as members of a community their subsequent silence/silencing is a cultural cryptonymy.

In a different coding of the crypt in and of language, Edwidge Danticat in *The Farming of Bones* addresses, first, the linguistic test that separated Haitians from their neighbours: the failure to pronounce the word for parsley, 'perejil', would immediately identify them as Haitians. Danticat writes:

> Many had heard rumours of groups of Haitians being killed in the night because they could not manage to trill their "r" and utter a throaty "j" to ask for parsley, to say perejil. (113–114)

Survival depends on the right turn of the tongue. Captured by a Dominican mob, Amabelle and her group are faced with this test:

> The young toughs waved parsley sprigs in front of our faces … 'Tell us what this is …'At that moment I did believe that had I wanted to I could have said the word properly, calmly, slowly, the way I often asked "perejil?" of the old Dominican women … even though the trill of the *r* and the precision of the

> / was sometimes too burdensome a joining for my tongue … But I didn't get my chance. Yves and I were shoved down into our knees. Our jaws were pried open and parsley stuffed into our mouths. (192–193)

The novel documents both, the enunciation (having to pronounce correctly) and the censoring with the Haitian mouths closed off with parsley. Danticat is pointing to, also, the absence of listeners even though Amabelle *could* have pronounced the word correctly. Defined by their linguistic ability but silenced in the languages they *could* speak in, the Haitians are massacred. More significantly, their stories cannot and will not be heard because 'their' language is never the current *language* of social justice. The crypt is, effectively, the Haitian language for Amabelle and her group because they are trapped in it, as are their memories of the massacre. This historical silencing of their experiences through a prohibition, or limitation, placed on their *enunciation* of these experiences is made forcefully by Danticat in several key passages. Yves comments to Amabelle about the Dominican efforts to document the Haitian survivors' stories: 'You tell the story, and then it's retold as they wish, written in words you do not understand, in a language that is theirs, not yours' (246). Yves is proposing that their stories have *a* language, but not an *acceptable* language to be enunciated in. Thus Man Rapadou, Yves' mother, tells Amabelle: 'I know your story.' Amabelle wonders: 'which story of mine did she know? Which story was she *told*?' (227, emphasis added).

Survivors in the hospital, writes Danticat, had a 'hunger to tell':

> Taking turns, they exchanged tales quickly, the haste in their voices sometimes blurring the words, for greater than their desire to be heard was the hunger to tell. One could hear it in the fervor of the declarations, the obscenities shouted when something could not be remembered fast enough, when a stutter allowed another speaker to race into his own account without the stutterer having completed his … Another group of voices argued for the right to speak next, as if their owners had been biting their tongues while this last man was speaking. (208–209)

Amabelle listening to these stories experiences a visceral reaction deep inside her: 'I felt my breath racing as if everything inside me was boiling' (209). However, Amabelle stays silent throughout this session of serialized, collective enunciation of communal trauma. Amabelle's silence, in contrast with the voluble enunciations of the other survivors, is metonymic of the encrypting of trauma, individual and collective. For a people condemned to torture and death because they cannot enunciate a word clearly, language is the crypt into which their lives are consigned. When given a chance, they exercise *their* language in order to bring to the surface the details in this crypt. This is why, towards the end of the novel, years after the massacre and the loss of Sebastien, Amabelle ponders on the need to speak, to bring to the surface, in and through language, what lies in the crypt. Danticat evokes the sense of encryption very clearly here:

> It is perhaps the great discomfort of those trying to silence the world to discover that we have voices sealed inside our heads, voices that with each passing day, grow even louder than the clamor of the world outside.
>
> The slaughter is the only thing that is mine enough to pass on. All I want to do is find a place to lay it down now and again, a safe nest where it will neither be scattered by the winds, nor remain forever buried beneath the sod. (265)

HR texts thus underscore the attempts to enunciate, decode and translate skeletons (*Anil's Ghost*), nightmares (Claude's in *Breaking the Tongue*), scars (*Waiting for the Barbarians*) or silences (*Bitter Fruit*, *Waiting for the Barbarians, The Farming of Bones*) as metonyms for exhuming the cultural crypts of a community. Being silenced, misinterpreted, misrepresented are all versions of being encrypted, suggests the HR text, and limit or open up the possibilities of mourning. It requires somebody to break the silence, as is the case with *Naming the Spirits* in which Cecilia publishes *The Wall*, her account of her imprisonment and torture. Thornton writes:

> Cecilia's words were loosening the tongues of readers who not long ago had hidden behind closed doors ... Cecilia's book released them from fear, untied the knots whose invisible strictures had bound their lips. (77)

It is almost as though a whole new language—testimony—has been unleashed with Cecilia's book. When Cecilia tells Gabriela in *Naming the Spirits* about her memoirs from prison, Gabriela asks her: 'a couple in my building lost their daughter. I was wondering if I should give them the book.' Cecilia replies: 'what happened to me, to my daughter, was part of a pattern. They might find some comfort in that' (98). Thornton suggests that in Cecilia's enunciation there might be other peoples' stories embedded, and thus the book becomes a visible sign of the crypt, the repressed memories of an entire community's many lives and deaths.

In some cases mourning is made possible at the level of the community because something emerges from the communal crypt, or mass grave. The silent girl in *Naming the Spirits* is an instance of the phantom-as-return-of-the-repressed. The girl, with eyes 'bright and vacant, inquiring and unfocussed' (27), is almost a phantom: 'the fact of the matter was that the girl should be dead, at least in a coma' (112). She also serves as a conduit for the spirits who are not only watching her, but also hoping she would be instrumental in their redemption, their return to 'visibility' in the form of exhumed bodies and the revelation of secret massacres. The spirits of the massacred narrate the events around their death in *Naming the Spirits*, in an admittedly heavy-handed narrative strategy, but which serves to literalize the phantomatic decrypting of a nation's secrets. (The nearly-dead Amabelle, likewise, is an unlikely survivor of the massacre in *The Farming of Bones*. Both, the unnamed girl and Amabelle represent the phantom, more dead than alive, more skeletal than fleshly.) The spirits actively encourage and speed on Cecilia's book:

> Because we had a stake in its success, we urged the drivers of delivery trucks to bypass favorite roadside hang-outs and press on, encouraging them to eat and drink on the move, because we knew how time worked, that it was like a wound in the flesh inexorably knitting itself together, forming scar tissue until the flesh forgets its violation. (79)

The reference to trauma—wounding—and healing in the above passage comes from ghosts, spirits of the massacre in the grove. Just as Cecilia's book is an attempt to prevent the 'war [from] receding further into the past' (66). To return to Gabriele Schwab again, 'the falsification or disregard of the past or the destruction and silencing of collective memories … is the breeding ground for the phantomatic return of shameful secrets on the level of individuals, families, communities, and possibly even nations' (57).

Yet phantoms also require a language when they emerge from the crypt to invert a national narrative. The silent, unnamed girl in *Naming the Spirits* finally regains some language: she identifies words, speaks them and can call out names. But the spirits of the massacred who hope this would cause the girl to identify the dead to their families are disappointed: 'it was as if she'd never heard us say who were in the quiet of the warehouse … they [the people who are caring for the girl] asked her who she was and that word never came' (117–118). A doctor identifies her condition as aphasia (129). Later she would insist that 'her name was not the only one that had been lost,' indicating a larger *number* of lost names (159).

Counterpublics

> People, the elder
> Might die
> of your forgetfulness.
> (Johannes Brobowski, 'Elderblossom', in Forché 447)

When the young are urged to forget, it erases the possibility of retaining specific memories that might then come to define the community itself. In Brobowski's verse this erasure is precisely what he cautions against, and thereby indicates the necessity of remembering.

HR texts propose a public haunted, as a community, by loss and pain, with memories of suffering and injustice. Such a public that defies, resists, subverts the official one constituted through sanctioned memories and narratives, comes into being in two ways in these texts.

Regimes of Memory

I have already noted how the disappeared occur and exist in narratives about them. These narratives offer the possibility of redemption and justice not through a return of the disappeared but through a reassignment, so to speak, to a larger collective memory that is beyond individual grief or a family's mourning. In this reassignment, we can see the emergence of a counterpublic, and it begins with memory.

When different regimes of memory are in operation, when memories come into conflict based on the need of the present, or when official memory projects (and memorializing) is at odds with the 'vernacular' memory project then the memory citizenship takes on a wholly different shape.

Novelized testimony, in addition to going a considerable way towards the reclamation of the subjectivity lost through torture or war, enables the making of a social self as well, which in turn enables the retrieval of the social ontology of the subject of HR. This is the effect of the narrators documenting 'sentiments that are socially circumscribed, confined to specific moments, situations, and speakers' (Plate 2008: 3).

The witness speaks in specific contexts in HR texts and this enables her/him to achieve a measure of agency. The witness is called upon, either by law or by social pressures, to speak. But what the witness brings to the occasion is not necessarily truth as legally admissible, but something more. The witness in the act of speaking or writing or rendering into some form accessible to the general public unleashes a discourse that exposes the hollowness of state discourses, the cracks in the political rhetoric of reconciliation and forgiveness. Invoking and evoking memories of secret prisons, producing a set of meanings about governance and the historical record.

Paul Sweetbread in Tony Eprile's *The Persistence of Memory* is gifted with total recall. Before testifying at the TRC regarding the actions of his army unit and its leader, Lyddie, in the midst of a ceasefire, on the Angolan border he is called upon to demonstrate his powers by recalling entire pages from the telephone directory (234–235). Lyddie, also testifying to the events, offers different memories, and the TRC hearings are then about determining which of these two to authenticate and believe. At one point a psychiatrist who had treated Sweetbread as a child offers his diagnosis that he (Sweetbread) 'suffers from delusions of memory' (259) and thereby discredits what he remembers of the war. Dirk Hendricks discredits Alex Mpondo in *Red Dust* by reminding him of how he, Alex, was happy once he had betrayed his comrades: 'You were so happy. Remember?' (193–194). Here again, different 'regimes of memory' (Radstone and Hodgkin 2003) are in operation: the victim who testifies is discredited so that a perpetrator might be granted clemency.

Michael Rothberg proposes that very often memories emerge 'in the interplay between different pasts and a heterogeneous present', or what he calls 'multidirectional memory', 'the interference, overlap, and mutual constitution of seemingly different collective memories' (2006: 162). This multidirectional memory helps constitute the public sphere in an entirely different way (162). Dissonant information arriving in the form of such multidirectional memory, argues Rothberg, produces a 'counterpublic', where 'embodied truth' comes into conflict with 'a certain formation of the bourgeois public sphere', revealing subtexts to existent and extant—official—memories (179). 'A counterpublic', proposes Rothberg, 'sets itself against the dominant by producing and circulating a stigmatized identity through forms that challenge the supposed neutrality and transparency of the general public sphere' (179). Extending Rothberg's argument about the undermining of the publics through dissonant information and multidirectional memory it is possible to also argue that structured discourses of reconciliation or 'acceptable' public memory in processes like the TRCs are also undermined. That is, the public formed around processes like TRCs and their 'truth telling' as well as official and normative (normalizing) discourses of the state are both undermined by dissident and embodied discourses from victims and sometimes from perpetrators. It constructs a publics that is essentially precarious and vulnerable.

I propose that HR texts in their examination of memory projects, regimes of memory and memory citizenship as constitutive of individual and communal identities often depict not only multidirectional memory but also memories that are at odds with the general publics.

Recounting the role of the state in the disappearances in *Imagining Argentina* the people gathered at Carlos' session construct an entirely different memory regime. This memory is of injury, loss and deprivation. In *The Truth Commissioner* the tape with Connor Walshe's voice revives memories even the public does not wish revived:

> Stanfield looks down on the listeners and sees their eyes drop to the floor as a kind of collective embarrassed shame settles on the room because they know they're listening to the voice of a boy who's about to die and they know their presence intrudes even all these years later and that their places should be taken by a priest or his family … they want the tape to stop. They don't want to hear the rest about how Fenton gave him money to supply information, of the places they met. They want the tape to finish. (328)

Despite James Fenton's attempts to not offer accurate information—he stonewalls with 'I don't remember' and 'I don't have a record' (329)—the voice of the dead boy forces Fenton to admit to the truth, eventually. If Fenton represents the regime of official and sanctioned memory, the boy's recorded voice represents an alternative one. Michael Madden is also advised to recall the events around Walshe's death in a particular way (333–336) but ends up narrating the events as they happened, taking recourse to his accurate and truthful memory of the events (337–340). If in *Red Dust* the politician Alex Mpondo is revealed as a subject who broke under torture and betrayed his cause, *The Truth Commissioner* has its Francis Gilroy, a former revolutionary and now Minister, who shot a boy dead.

In each of these cases the memories of violence and suffering render the public sphere at once sentimental and unstable. People in authority lose their social standing, and some, like Pieter Muller in *Red Dust*, have cases filed against them. Processes like the TRCs, as we can see in HR texts such as the above, become sites of contest between regimes of remembering and forgetting. In many cases the 'recall' is cast as 'confessional scripts' that 'allow perpetrators to reinvent their past through narrative' (Payne 19). Dirk Hendricks' supposed recall of the interrogation of Mpondo and Sizela in *Red Dust* is a case in point. Here Hendricks, like Fenton in *The Truth Commissioner*, reinvents a past and a self for his own purposes: a past in which he merely followed orders, lost his own family, is traumatized by the actions that he, as a conscientious police officer perpetrated. Hendricks first informs the TRC of his own loss: his wife has asked him for a divorce (127–128). Later he explains:

> I was a loyal policeman. We were taught that the enemy was all around, that we must fight communism and its terrorists with all our might. This is what I did. I did not benefit financially from my actions … I did it for the good of South Africa … We were in a war situation. People do all kinds of terrible things in wartime.' (130–131)

We see an exact replica of Hendricks' self-reinvention as part of his recall in Fenton's statements in *The Truth Commissioner*:

> Things were falling apart, society was falling apart. When you reported on duty you never knew what was going to happen, what you might have to deal with. People were dying. Men, women … and children, too. We were in a war, things change in a war. Things happen that shouldn't happen. (331)

Sarath Diyasena, seeking to mitigate the threat to his, and Anil's, lives as a result of her public accusations against the state in *Anil's Ghost*, suggests that their society needs peace and not the chaos brought on by specific kinds of memory, aided, in this case, by forensic archaeology (275).

Perpetrator and victim memories, such as cited above, construct a different public sphere. It humanizes perpetrators such as Hendricks and Fenton by revealing supposed gaps in their private memories, suggesting that they are as prone to forgetting as anybody else. But the key feature of HR texts is that they position these acts of recall and forgetting as attempts to deflect the making-public of private memories. For instance, when the policeman is asked about his torture of victims in *Red Dust* or *Of Love and Shadows*, the response 'I don't remember' needs to be read as a regime of memory that seeks to ensure the continued invisibility of private memory from the public gaze. The irony of such acts of wilful amnesia and continued invisibilizing is that, as Leigh Payne observes, 'when perpetrators say "I cannot remember", they hint at a truth ... They do not deny, they fail to remember' (249). Payne adds: 'partial memory or explanations of memory loss without denial ... lead audiences to doubt these confessions' (249).

The HR text by highlighting such incidents of forgetting point towards the regime of memory that seeks to keep the private memories of torturers, killers and jailors out of the public gaze but ends up constructing a public sphere around the doubt instilled in the audience by such public admissions of forgetting-without-denial. Further, individual perpetrators like Hendricks, Fenton, Ramirez (in *Of Love and Shadows*) and others, offer amnesia and justification but *not* denials of the events. If this implies something horrific did indeed happen in the prison or camp and therefore, such statements by perpetrators result not in a collective amnesia but a remembering—evidenced materially in some cases by Mpondo—of the excesses. *That is, we are looking at a regime of memory, a public or communitarian one, of disappearances, deaths and tortures that is not only* not *denied by the wilful amnesia of perpetrators but strengthened when they admit, rather naïvely, to a mere 'not remembering'.* The regime of public memory of the *truth* of torture is at odds with the regime of memory that causes perpetrators to forget what they did and is oddly reinforced by institutionalized mechanisms of recall such as TRCs.

Loss, Absence and Inquiry

Raami in *In the Shadow of the Banyan* wonders: 'We didn't even know where Papa had been taken, where he might have last been seen ... Where was his grave? Did he have a grave?' (309). Just as Raami seeks the body, or information about the body, of her father, HR texts yield numerous characters in quest of their loved ones. These novels are primarily texts where the subject of human rights is absent, the *habeas corpus* invalidated and families and communities left with nothing except absent presences. In Crimean poet Abba Kovner's 'What's Not in the Heart' a survivor recalls a loved one. There is no evidence of what happened to this loved one, and the survivor can only bear the evidence of memory:

> Only your returning shadow
> exists. My hands will never
> Touch you. Your coffin
> Never leaves my shoulders.
> (In Forché 543)

The survivor is defined by the loss of the loved one, with no accurate knowledge of what happened to the loved one.

The absent body of Sirissa (*Anil's Ghost*), Sisowath (*In the Shadow of the Banyan*), Teresa (and several others in *Imagining Argentina*), Ling-li (*Breaking the Tongue*) and Susana (*Requiem for a Woman's Soul*) symbolize in Rachel Cyr's words an 'affirmation of a truth without having to equate it with knowledge' (2013: 104). Cyr continues:

> [the empty tomb must be seen] not as absence but as a loss that cannot be verified according to certain rules, the testimony founded sometimes on trust and faith and phrased in a memorial genre where the archival, the biological, and even indexical "assert nothing" but where the witness must assert the event nonetheless. (104)

The witness asserts the event of loss, in the face of an absence of any evidence, and establishes a commonality with other such witnesses. The denial of closure that results from an absence of the 'body of evidence' is a form of truth that exists independent of evidentiary knowledge, and to which the community bears witness. For Ananda, Amabelle, Carlos and the numerous other survivors in HR texts there is neither justice nor redemption. Yet there exists for them *a truth*: of loss. The crowds waiting for the Justice of the Peace in *The Farming of Bones*, the audience at the TRC in *The Truth Commissioner* and *Red Dust*, the audience at Carlos' sessions in *Imagining Argentina*, the families in the town square in *Of Love and Shadows* share *loss*.

I propose that in HR texts we can see the formation of a public sphere around this *truth* of loss rather than juridical and legally admissible *knowledge*, or even the idea of justice. Loss is a truth that all communities in HR texts live with, on a daily basis. This public sphere is built around a specific kind of narrative and communicative action that deals with loss. The HR text ponders over the missing body, the absent and empty grave. It links the sense of loss in the lives of survivors with the absent bodies and/or evidence. The HR text further proposes that such an absence of material, documentary, verbal and official *information* about the lost 'bodies' of loved ones contributes to the new order of the public itself by initiating a new narrative mode, the inquiry.

In *Imagining Argentina* the Mothers at the Plaza wait with placards bearing questions addressed to the state:

> WHERE IS RUBEN MACIAS?
> WHERE IS JULIA OBREGON?
> WHERE HAVE YOU TAKEN MY DAUGHTER AND GRANDSON? (37)

Carlos goes to meet General Guzman about his missing wife, Cecilia, and the nuns. After looking through a 'list of subversives', Guzman declares: 'There is no record … their names are not on the list so they have not committed any crimes' (106–107). Connor Walshe's mother and sister appealing to Henry Stanfield, the Chairman of the TRC, regarding their boy's disappearance tell him how when they enquired with the authorities, they are simply sent away with falsehoods like 'he was living in Dublin or England' (Park 29). In *Of Love and Shadows* Isabel Allende writes about a family's search for information about their missing sons:

> For months they made the obligatory pilgrimage of anyone following the trail of *desaparecidos*. They went from place to place, asking futile questions, and received nothing but the advice to consider the men dead … papers were lost in offices in the capital. (253)

When the unnamed General in *Of Love and Shadows* is told by his subordinates 'they keep asking about their *desaparecidos*', he responds with 'tell them we don't know whether they're alive or dead' (280).

Clearly then, there is no accurate information forthcoming from the state or the legal machinery about their loss. The inquiry as a narrative mode of the subject people and community about loss comes into being when official narratives that offer explanations are essentially absences: an absence of information, an absence of material evidence and the absence of an identifiable perpetrator.

A public, as Michael Warner has defined it, is 'the social space created by the reflexive circulation of discourse'. It is 'understood to be an ongoing space of encounter for discourse' and 'exists only by virtue of address' (2002: 61–62). Michael Rothberg's definition, already cited, suggests that a counterpublic emerges with the circulation of discourses of 'stigmatized identity' (179). If one adds to this the kind of inquiry about loss and injury, then we see an entirely new discursive regime, and therefore a public, coming into being.

Amabelle in *The Farming of Bones* inquires with other survivors arriving from Santiago as to the whereabouts of her lover, Sebastien, and his sister. Amabelle's letter to Doctor Javier asks:

> I would be most grateful for your guidance as to where to find Michehne Onius and Sebastien Onius, who are said to have perished in Santiago at the time of the slaughter. Desiring to know if you have seen and know this to be true. (255)

Other survivors too ask for information about their missing families: 'has he come, my son? Have they come, my daughter, my man, my woman, my mother, my father?' (205). Armen in *Sandcastle Girls* searches the 'convoys of dying women for anyone who can tell him anything more about where and how his wife and young daughter most likely perished' (37). He does little else besides 'wait[ing] for the convoys … always hoping to find a group from Harput in which there might be someone who can tell him something more about the day his wife and daughter were herded into the convoy' (43). The Sizelas in *Red Dust* and Raami *In the Shadow of the Banyan* seek information about their missing ones from their neighbourhoods, friends and others as a response to the official silence or denial around the disappearances. Carlos, holding 'sessions' in which he has visions of the missing persons, is under pressure by the families of missing people, to provide accurate information about, first, whether those missing are alive or dead, and second, if alive, where they might be.

I propose that the non-official inquiry as a narrative form is what brings the people of a community together. The inquiry is a form of address to the state and to its apparatus (the police, the government, the secret service) from the community. This narrative is in contrast to the official inquiries, or even the transitional justice apparatuses with their own inquiries (such as TRCs). In the place of the rational debate and conversations that make up the traditional public sphere, the HR novel posits the sorrowful and anxious inquiry and exchange of information as a mode of mobilizing both the public and public sentiments. This communicative action of inquiries and hearsay constitutes a response to the indifferent official space, and is a counterpublic.

Notes

1. There is a sense in the uncanny of the 'secret encounter', an 'apprehension … of something that should have remained secret and hidden has come to light' (Royle 2003: 2).
2. Attempts to identify the dead in mass graves have been a part of memory projects in various parts of the world. Associations like Asociación para la Recuperación de la Memoria Histórica (Association for the Recovery of Historical Memory) in Spain, for instance, have been exhuming bodies and carrying out DNA testing to identify the dead and connect them to the survivor families.

Bibliography

Abraham, Nicolas, and Mária Török. 1986. *The Wolf Man's Magic Word: A Cryptonymy*. Minneapolis: University of Minnesota Press.

Agamben, Giorgio. 1998. *Homo Sacer: Sovereign Power and Bare Life*. Trans. Daniel Heller-Roazen. Stanford: Stanford University Press.

Althey, Stephanie. 2012. Dark Chamber, Colonial Scene: Post-9/11 Torture and Representation. In *Theoretical Perspectives on Human Rights and Literature*, ed. Elizabeth Swanson Goldberg, and Alexandra Schultheis Moore, 180–197. New York: Routledge.

Cyr, Rachel E. 2013. Testifying Absence in the Era of Forensic Testimony. *International Journal Politics Culture Society* 26: 93–106.

Dawes, James. 2007. *That the World May Know: Bearing Witness to Atrocity*. Cambridge, MA: Harvard University Press.

Ghosh, Bishnupriya. 2004. On Grafting the Vernacular: The Consequences of Postcolonial Spectrology. *Boundary 2* 31(2): 197–218.

Johnson, Peter. 2013. The Geographies of Heterotopia. *Geography Compass* 7(11): 790–803.

Kleinman, Arthur, Veena Das and Margaret Lock (ed). 1997. *Social Suffering*. Berkeley, CA: University of California Press.

Kontsevaia, Diana B. 2013. Mass Graves and the Politics of Reconciliation: Construction of Memorial Sites After the Srebrenica Massacre. *Totem* 21(1): 13–31.

Lovell, Julia. 2006. Review of Vyvyane Loh, *Breaking the Tongue*. *The Guardian*, June 24. http://www.theguardian.com/books/2006/jun/24/featuresreviews.guardianreview19. Accessed 17 Sep 2015.

Mbembe, Achille. 2003. Necropolitics. Trans. Libby Meintjes. *Public Culture* 15(1): 11–40.

Payne, Leigh A. 2008. *Unsettling Accounts: Neither Truth Nor Reconciliation in Confessions of State Violence*. Durham and London: Duke University Press.

Perera, Suvendrini. 2006. "They Give Evidence": Bodies, Borders and the Disappeared. *Social Identities* 12(6): 637–656.

Plate, Liedeke. 2008. Bearing Witness: Gender and the Poetry of 9/11. *Women's Studies* 37: 1–16.

Pollack, Craig Evan. 2003. Intentions of Burial: Mourning, Politics, and Memorials Following the Massacre at Srebrenica. *Death Studies* 27: 125–142.

Radstone, Susanna and Katharine Hodgkin (ed). 2003. *Regimes of Memory.* London and New York: Routledge.

Rothberg, Michael. 2006. Between Auschwitz and Algeria: Multidirectional Memory and the Counterpublic Witness. *Critical Inquiry* 33(1): 158–184.

Royle, Nicholas. 2003. *The Uncanny.* Manchester: Manchester University Press.

Salgado, Minoli. 2013. Vanishing Points/Visible Fictions: The Textual Politics of Terror. *Textual Practice* 27(2): 207–223.

Scheper-Hughes, Nancy. 2002. Coming to Our Senses: Anthropology and Genocide. In *Annihilating Difference: The Anthropology of Genocide*, ed. Alexander Hinton, 348–381. Berkeley and Los Angeles, CA: University of California Press.

Schwab, Gabriele. 2010. *Haunting Legacies: Violent Histories and Transgenerational Trauma.* New York: Columbia University Press.

Sturken, Marita. 1997. Absent Images of Memory: Remembering and Reenacting the Japanese Internment. *Positions* 5(3): 687–707.

Tyner, James A. 2014. Dead Labor, Landscapes, and Mass Graves: Administrative Violence During the Cambodian Genocide. *Geoforum* 52: 70–77.

Waller, James. 2002. *Becoming Evil: How Ordinary People Commit Genocide and Mass Killing.* New York: Oxford University Press.

Conclusion: From Generalizability to Ethical Literacy

This conclusion proposes the idea of 'ethical literacy' that may be generated from a reading of HR texts.

This book has examined literary texts from around the world in order to see representations of HR violations and their effects. The emphasis here has been on what Domna Stanton has described as 'generalizable', 'a process without end—generalizabilization—for forging commonalities' (2016: 32). Stanton cites Foucault when she speaks of 'infinitesimal local mechanisms' that then move upward in an ascending manner toward more general mechanisms (32).

Literary texts, this book suggests, reveal states and processes that are generalizable: from the unmaking of bodies and collapsing social worlds to witnessing and the making of counterpublics. By tracking these across various texts emerging from diverse social, economic and cultural contexts—Dalits in India, apartheid in South Africa, the Armenian massacres, Sarajevo during war time, Argentina and Chile under military rule, Sri Lankan civil war, theocratic Iran, Singapore and Korea during World War II, among others—the book builds up generalizable conditions and processes of torture, witnessing and public-formations.

Focusing on such generalizable conditions and processes via their literary representations enables one to foreground the role of humanities, and literary studies within the humanities, in constructing *models* of humanity, life and their vulnerability in various contexts. When we examine

P.K. Nayar, *Human Rights and Literature*,
DOI 10.1057/978-1-137-50432-6

the emergence of counterpublics and practices of mourning that build communities, we then in literary studies also focus on the struggles—and resistance—of and within these communities to come to terms with their pasts, and the *expression* of these struggles. These expressions provide the vocabulary of Human Rights that work *outside* literature too: of pain, eroding social ontologies (Turner 2006) of the human in diverse societies, the notion of a 'person', mourning and memory and finally, justice.

Such studies are crucial for the vocabulary they generate but also as forms of advocacy. Sophia McClennen and Alexandra Schultheis Moore write in their introduction to the *Routledge Companion to Literature and Human Rights*:

> The use of literature as a vehicle for human rights advocacy is at once a way to illuminate the humanity of the speaking subject as it is a mode of reflecting a "story" that has been erased by official "history". Literature functions as a source of struggle, thereby challenging the presumed western overemphasis on history as a claim to authenticity. (2016: 12)

Whether the novel or the play is the appropriate form in which violations, resilience, recovery and resistance might be conveyed as a counterpoint to 'history' remains a matter of debate, instanced in the volumes of critical studies of HR and literature with sections devoted to forms.

That literature is able to 'expose' those acts and processes that have been driven underground, both literally in the sense of spaces of massacres and tortures being displaced to hidden sites and figuratively in the sense of the silence of historical records, is what generates its crucial role in the HR regime. That is, literature makes the subject of torture—in the double sense of the victim of torture but also torture as a subject of discussion—a constituent of *common* knowledge, a *shared* vocabulary and a *circulatable* discourse. It is in its ability to represent the 'dark chamber' (Coetzee's name for the torture chamber, 1999), literature makes visible those stories that have been edited, redacted or plain silenced. In this sense, literary representations of HR violations constitute a domain wherein what could not previously be narrated makes it appearance. Joseph Slaughter writing about visual representations of torture uses Prince's idea of the unnarrated—that which, 'according to a given narrative, cannotbe narrated or is not worth narrating' (Prince, cited in Slaughter 2016: 115)—to claim that declassified documents are crucial for HR: the declassified documents, the unnarrated, which was once narrated, 'draws attention to itself as a political absence' (115). However, this Slaughter reading hinges on a pre-existing, presumably complete document that was censored and redacted and which is *now* available in its sanitized form, with large swathes of the unnarrated.

Yet much of HR literature offers a different *sense* of the unnarrated. Literary texts such as the ones discussed here represent those dark chambers in the life of a nation and its people about which no narrative is possible except from those who lived and died in the narration: because those who narrated from the dark chambers were either victims or perpetrators. Characteristic of much literary fiction around HR violations is the death or 'muting' of the victim-witness. In Lawrence Thornton's *Naming the Spirits* the sole survivor of a massacre has become a mute. *Anil's Ghost* concludes with the voice of Sarat, who is presumably dead, emanating from a cassette clandestinely smuggled to Anil, literally a voice from the grave. In *Requiem for a Woman's Soul* Susana writes in pain and in a practically indecipherable script that Father Antonio, the recipient of these texts, has to carefully interpret and translate. Eventually, Antonio himself is driven to insanity and the novel concludes with him mumbling 'unintelligible words' (Epilogue). In *Breaking the Tongue* Ling-li, now dead, 'calls' to Claude in his dream and asks him to return to prison so that he might record the manner in which she was tortured: 'If you won't remember and record this, who will? This is how our history starts and is transmitted. Witness and transmission of Story' (p. 480). In *Imagining Argentina* Carlos shares the visions he has of the events around the disappeared with their families, as though there is no narrative other than these visions. Far too many texts offer literal and metaphoric disappearance of language and narrative around the dissolving subject of HR for it to be mere coincidence. Such texts that devote themselves to the 'voice' of the muted gesture at not just the unnarrated at the heart of the nation or social order, but the disnarrated.

Gerald Prince (1988) speaks of 'all the events that *do not* happen but, nonetheless, are referred to (in a negative or hypothetical mode) by the narrative text' as the disnarrated (2–3). Prince lists the following as instances of the disnarrated in narrative:

> Expressions of impossibility or unrealized possibility, deontic expressions of observed prohibition, epistemic expressions of ignorance, ontologic expressions of nonexistence, purely imagined worlds, desired worlds or intended worlds, unfulfilled expectations, unwarranted beliefs, failed expectations, crushed hopes, suppositions and false calculations, errors and lies.

One feature of literary texts documenting violations is the disbelief expressed within the text by other characters about the events that befell the narrator. In *Red Dust* the policeman Hendricks disputes that torture was inflicted upon Alex. For Paul Sweetbread in *The Persistence of Memory*, his eidetic memory about the violence he witnessed is mocked, questioned and eventually dismissed as a madman's delusions. In *War Trash* the army camp does not believe that the Korean women have been raped and then converted into prostitutes by the invading army. In *Imagining Argentina* the crowds who come to listen to Carlos 'seeing' the victims in his visions are often uncertain about the events he narrates. In *Waiting for the Barbarians*, nobody believes the Magistrate when he claims the so-called barbarians are victims and not predatorial rebels against the Empire. Those who read the victim narratives are themselves stunned into madness or silence, as noted earlier in the case of Rivabella's text. Lucy does not wish to speak about her rape in *Disgrace*, exactly in the same fashion as Lydia in *Bitter Fruit*.

Since nobody, or very few, believe(s) the narration of the tortures or humiliation, the entire victim-narrative itself is the symbol of the documentation of what may have happened but didn't, in the eyes of the disbelieving narratees in the texts. In other words, the disnarrated emerges within the rhetoric of disbelief, silence and scepticism that frames the victim and her/his in HR texts. We as readers thus engage with the text precisely because there is silence, madness, scepticism and counterarguments about and against the victim narratives *within* the HR texts. The disnarrated is what makes the HR text powerful in terms of how extreme events that befall individuals become sites of contestation within the narrative but which then 'slow down' (Prince's term) *our* reading to ponder: if these events did not happen, why does the narrator mention it? (Vindrola-Pedros and Johnson 2014). The disnarrated depicts, in Prince's formulation, 'what is not or what might be'. The disnarrated is, then, a narration of events as experienced by victims, but a narration contested within the narrative by sceptics, disputatious legal mechanisms and others, and yet draws our attention to the structures of storytelling. The disnarrated is an important aspect of HR discourse because it serves as a meta-critical strategy by forcing us to see how victim-narratives are dismissed as improbable, as never-having-happened or even delusional. The silences enforced through such dismissals in the narratives serve, therefore, as a comment on the way victim voices are silenced outside in the HR campaigns as well. I see the disnarrated that emerges in HR texts as a key component of HR advocacy because of this function.

The disnarrated within the literature of HR enables a social imaginary about the vulnerable human, whose sustaining environments have collapsed, who witnesses the destruction of fellow subjects and whose claim to subjecthood is often through a reiteration of the trauma s/he experienced or participation in memory projects. HR literature, then, fits into a demand made of contemporary HR discourse: 'human rights need *redirecting* towards the embodied, vulnerable human being' (Grear 2010: 3, emphasis in original). The HR literary text is integral to the project of human rights because it demonstrates how broken bodies are produced in eroding social conditions, driven by state policy, state indifference or state oppression. Coming out of different cultural and political contexts, the authors of such fiction all fit a pattern when they focus on conditions of institutional precarity as generating the broken subject.

Stories that offer us accounts of torture or repression from the point of view of the victim—as most HR texts are wont to do—deliver to us readers the *person* who suffers. Abuse, debasement, pain, deprivation, witnessing and traumatic recall in the HR texts help us to develop a portrait of the person who has suffered. It enables us to perceive a self that has been eroded, but has documented its erosion. They are crucial for giving us ideas about the human person. These stories therefore are crucial in democratizing ideas about human dignity and its potential repression at the hands of the state.

More importantly, I see HR literature's social imaginary as providing a framework to understand similar (but not identical) atrocities in the *contemporary*. Atrocity, war and violation narratives such as the ones discussed in this book should be read beyond their immediate spatial-temporal context—Korea, Singapore or Chile, the Armenian massacre, 1975 Argentina, the Second World War, and so on—as constitutive of an essential cultural memory that enables us to see, in particular, the imminent arrival of similar atrocities in the present. Thus, HR literature is one that expands beyond its immediate contexts to generate an ethical frame for reading, say, vulnerability, in the contemporary as well. To read literature about the Holocaust—often the transcendent signifier for all things inhuman—is to develop such frames to read about the Sri Lankan civil war, the situation in Syria or Nigeria.

These frames might be described as literacies: around vulnerable bodies, social ontologies, unmaking worlds for us to locate the contemporary within these, with all these literacies being constitutive of a larger ethical literacy. This, finally, is what HR literature helps construct: an awareness of how we read texts about violations, the appropriate response to these texts and the linkage of these texts to advocacy in the present. When we move beyond the immediate text to link it to the context of contemporary suffering and violations we work toward the *generalizability* of the vulnerable without sacrificing the local and the particular. Ethical literacy is an expansion of the immediate text to the generalizable conditions to be found within the text, the ethical frame drawn from the text to be applied to the contemporary. It is this generalizability that would, if we could, make ethical readers as well.

Bibliography

Coetzee, J.M. 1999. *Disgrace*. London: Secker and Warburg.

Grear, Anna. 2010. *Redirecting Human Rights: Facing the Challenge of Corporate Legal Humanity*. London: Palgrave Macmillan.

McClennen, Sophia, and Alexandra Schultheis Moore. 2016. Introduction: Aporia and Affirmative Critique. In *The Routledge Companion to Literature and Human Rights*, ed. Sophia McClennen, and Alexandra Schultheis Moore, 1–19. New York: Routledge.

———. 2016. Vanishing Points: When Narrative is Simply Not There. In *The Routledge Companion to Literature and Human Rights*, ed. Sophia McClennen, and Alexandra Schultheis Moore, 109–125. New York: Routledge.

Prince, Gerald. 1988. The Disnarrated. *Style* 22(1): 1–8.

Stanton, Domna. 2016. A New Universal for Human Rights? The Particular, the Generalizable, the Political. In *The Routledge Companion to Literature and Human Rights*, ed. Sophia McClennen, and Alexandra Schultheis Moore, 27–36. New York: Routledge.

Turner, Bryan S. 2006. *Vulnerability and Human Rights*. University Park: University of Pennsylvania Press.

Vindrola-Pedros, Cecilia, and Ginger Johnson. 2014. The Narrated, Nonnarrated, and the Disnarrated: Conceptual Tools for Analyzing Narratives in Health Services Research. *Qualitative Health Research* 24(11): 1603–1611.

Index

P.K. Nayar, *Human Rights and Literature*,
DOI 10.1057/978-1-137-50432-6

www.ingramcontent.com/pod-product-compliance
Lightning Source LLC
LaVergne TN
LVHW010319220926
848484LV00004BB/802

* 9 7 8 1 1 3 7 5 0 4 3 1 9 *